Praise for *Real Followers:*

This is a "spit and mu
found way of thinking
work of Christ.

—*John Savage, D. Min.,*
President of Lead Consultants Corporation,
Reynoldsburg, Ohio

This book's wisdom will help one hundred thousand Christians to venture deep, experience abundant life, and make a difference.

—*George G. Hunter, III, Dean,*
E. Stanley Jones School of World Mission and Evangelism

The moving story of a pastor who was not content just seeing the fields in his parish ready for harvest. Invigorating reading! A challenging addition to the contemporary church growth literature.

—*Robert E. Coleman*
Director of the School of World Mission and Evangelism

Michael Slaughter's book will inspire you and fellow believers to go where God created us to go—to be a part of the "Fourth Great Awakening" of the Christian church. You will want to make significant, personal changes through the life-transforming power of Jesus Christ.

—*Florence Littauer,*
Speaker and Author of 30 books

Mike Slaughter cuts through the "pretend" posture of the modern church and offers a prescription for wholeness in Christ.

—*Max Williams, Pastor,*
Liworth United Methodist Church, Worthington, Ohio

Michael Slaughter poignantly and powerfully points out why virtual Christianity can never achieve what can be achieved through the real thing, i.e., vital connection with Jesus Christ. Michael reveals in fresh, understandable language the challenges, cost, and compensation of being vitally connected to Jesus Christ.

—*Joey Johnson, Senior Pastor, The House of the Lord*

It's time to abandon cultural Christianity and become Real Followers of Jesus. Michael Slaughter tells us what that looks like and how to do it. Must reading for serious disciples of Jesus.

—*Jim Tomberlin, Senior Pastor,*
Woodmen Valley Chapel, Colorado Springs

Our generation has had its fill of "pretend Christianity" and is crying for the real thing. In typical Slaughter fashion, *Real Followers* urges every Christian to fill that gap and go one step beyond comfort. Without question this book will provoke you to examine your own followership.

—*Tim Schroeder, Kelowna, British Columbia, Canada*

Impressive. Slaughter has not only identified the bull's-eye for ministry of discipleship, but hit it consistently. There are few leaders in the Christian church who fully understand and capitalize on the needs for authenticity and integrity in the Christian walk. Slaughter does.

—*Michael W. Foss, Prince of Peace Lutheran Church,*
St. Paul, Minnesota

Good leaders are "boxing the air" without good followers. Here's a book that will not only help Christians be better members. It will help members be better Christians.

—*Dr. Charles Arn, President,*
Church Growth, Inc. (Monrovia, CA)

Real Followers leaves not room for escape. This gripping call to move beyond "safe and calculated lives" requires an immediate heart response; no "virtual" responses will suffice.

—*G. John Baergen, Executive Director,*
The International Centre for Leadership
Development and Evangelism

Real Followers

Beyond Virtual Christianity

Michael Slaughter

with Warren Bird

Abingdon Press
Nashville

REAL FOLLOWERS:
BEYOND VIRTUAL CHRISTIANITY

Copyright © 1999 by Abingdon Press

All rights reserved.

This book is printed on recycled, acid-free, elemental-chlorine–free paper.

Library of Congress Cataloging-in-Publication Data

Slaughter, Michael.
    Real followers: beyond virtual Christianity/Michael Slaughter with Warren Bird.
      p. cm.
    ISBN 0-687-03341-1 (alk. paper)
    1. Christian life.   I. Bird, Warren.   II. Title.
    BV4501.2.S4765   1999
    248.4—dc21   99-42546
                                              CIP

99 00 01 02 03 04 05 06 07 08 — 10 9 8 7 6 5 4 3 2 1

MANUFACTURED IN THE UNITED STATES OF AMERICA

Acknowledgments

You might say this book has been more than a hundred years in the making. That's because it wouldn't be possible without the many God moments that have made **Ginghamsburg Church,** founded in 1863, what it is today. The evidence of God's Spirit at work in this faith community gives the book its credibility and relevance.

I was appointed as Ginghamsburg's pastor in 1979. I wouldn't trade anything for the experiences and friendships of my years there. The pages that follow introduce only a small number of the exciting stories of life change that have taken place as people have learned what it means to become **real followers of Jesus.**

I thank my wife, **Carolyn,** and children, **Kristen** and **Jonathan,** who have been vulnerable enough to allow me to print stories from our family life and from their own lives.

Real Followers has been a team effort. The ministry of Ginghamsburg Church takes place through small groups and teams. This book is immeasurably better because of the team that shaped its original form as worship celebrations, and then also its adapted form as a book. Many ideas came from our **worship design team**, consisting primarily of **Kim Miller, Len Wilson, Francis Wyatt, Jason Moore, Mike Lyons,** with whom I live out my call from week to week.

Some of those team members critiqued the manuscript, while other readers are longtime friends in the congregation. In that regard, I want to especially thank the following for their time and help with the first drafts of the book: **Tammy Kelley, Kim Miller, Donna McGraw, John Jung, John Ward,** and **Carolyn Slaughter**. **Mike Lyons** and **Jane Moresi** have also given advice and valuable assistance.

Ginghamsburg Church's Director of Cyberministry is **Mark Stephenson.** He has coordinated efforts to put on the Internet illustrated transcriptions, audios, and videos of our worship events and conferences. The *http:www.ginghamsburg.org* site not only benefits literally thousands of people each month from around the globe, but as a side benefit, the background work greatly assisted the editorial process of this book. Besides Mark, some of the most heavily involved members of the cyberministry, transcription, and web graphics teams are **Steve Curtis, Pamela Neveu, Jerry Warner, Carolyn Slaughter, Mary Ross, Linda Dean, Ginny Patterson, Pat Hedleston,** and **Jason Moore.**

Warren Bird and I first met in early 1991 when he interviewed me on behalf of one of my mentors, Carl George. Warren and I have done several projects together over the years. Warren's collaborative role on this book has enabled me to keep my focus on what's ahead for Ginghamsburg Church, and not rob my family of time away from them. Anything you don't like about the book is Warren's fault (just kidding).

I give everything I am and have to the **Lord Jesus Christ,** knowing that whatever worthwhile I have to say is because the Spirit has invaded my very being.

Contents

Do you want to be part of a God movement? You need to be challenged to take God at face value. But you can't make this journey alone. You need the camaraderie of a faith community that is significantly engaged in contemporary culture but not sold out to it. You will find help from a radical community of real followers who get honest with God.

God still speaks today. In fact, God is speaking now. When God moves, are you willing to move? When God stops, are you willing to stop? Are you ready?

A Foreword for All Readers

Occasionally, a book comes along that truly surprises us. It blindsides us. It churns our stagnant souls. It jumpstarts the kind of raw self-searching we normally save for dark and sleepless nights or for those crisis moments when sin, selfishness, and meaninglessness explode like searing magma through the cracks of our lives.

Real Followers is that kind of a book. If you choose to read it, whether individually or in an adult small group study, you won't have to slog through umpteen sleepless nights in order to get a good look at yourself. Nor do you have to wait for a crisis of volcanic proportions. *Real Followers* is as good a spiritual seismograph as you'll ever hope to find.

That said, let's just get clear about what this book is *not*. Given the fact that Mike Slaughter is the lead pastor

11

of Ginghamsburg United Methodist Church—one of the fastest growing congregations in the United States—*Real Followers* easily could have been a "How-to-Build-a-Megachurch-in-a-Cornfield" manual, or a "We-Did-It-You-Can-Do-It-Too" course, complete with enough charts, strategies, and five-year plans to ensure nausea. It could have been a smug "Pulled-Myself-Up-by-My-Bootstraps" autobiography of an ecclesiastical entrepreneur. It could also have been a "How-to-Be-a-Christian-in-the-Suburbs-Without-Totally-Messing-Up-Your-Life" guide.

Michael Slaughter helps us see why *Real Followers* is none of the above. "I become concerned when churches, including Ginghamsburg, grow bigger. I don't want growth that leaves people unchanged—virtual followers who exist in effect, but not in fact. I want us to be the 'real deal'—real followers of Jesus. I want to lead us away from self-realization and toward God-realization."

At the turn of the millennium, self-gratification is the assumed purpose of every human being. Addiction is normative. Unbridled consumption seems to have been stamped indelibly into our genetic code. And, of course, image is everything—which is why "Let's pretend" isn't just for preschoolers anymore. It is now very much an adult game, only, it has a new name: "Let's compartmentalize." And this new game has been cultivated into an art form, from cyber space to public space.

None of us has a choice as to *when* we live. But we all have a choice as to *how* we live. Do you and I respond to our "now" by retreating into laissez-faire churchianity? Do we settle for virtual piety, a go-through-the-motions display, forgetting that Jesus' bedrock requirement for discipleship is quite simply, "Love me with your life"? (paraphrase, John 14:21).

Mike Slaughter and the real followers at Ginghamsburg Church have made a different choice. They have courageously broken stride with virtual, self-serving religion. In essence, they have provided a living course-correction to the last two decades of "Christianity Lite." Their stories are those of ordinary people who made one simple decision: they decided to let God invade and radically remold their lives. And the effect is astonishing: *It is the church as you've probably never seen it. But the church you always dreamed could be.*

Real Followers is compelling, visceral, grace-filled reading. But, more than anything, this book is dangerous reading, whether you read it individually or in an adult small group study. Read it and be willing to risk life as you know it.

Sally Morgenthaler
Lay Worship Leader
Author, *Worship Evangelism*
Littleton, Colorado

A Foreword for Pastors

Warning: This book is not mild-mannered, business-as-usual, arms-length stuff. To get a flavor, simply look at the table of contents.  I don't read very many books all the way through. This one is so compelling that I finished it, and did so in two sittings. Both the content and the way it was presented captured my attention.

Here's why. A fresh season in American Christianity is now in its beginning phase. I call it the Third Wave. The book you are about to read characterizes it as well as anything I have seen. If you want to discover the spirit and essence of this new era, *Real Followers* provides a good medium for doing so.

The first wave of American Christianity was one of *replication*. The church in the United States started as an import from Europe. Immigrants from British Methodist, German Lutheran, and other parishes simply relocated them onto American soil. Many of those transplants are still with us today. Their central values include tradition, ritual, and preservation of their rich heritage. They are quickly recognized by their European architecture, classical music, and—at least at the Episcopal church where I grew up as a young adult—pretty much the same liturgy as what was being used in England.

The second wave, now at its apex, is *proclamation*. Churches like this create an experience that is analogous to a concert or sports gathering. The big-crowd event itself is a main thing, whether a Billy Graham preaching mission, Robert Schuller's "Hour of Power" telecast, or a worship service at one of today's megachurches. The proclamation wave is like a broadcast medium for the most part. The message travels primarily one way as the central person plays the role of the great communicator: preacher, actor, musician, or teacher. It's enthusiastic and participatory. It's a grand and very high-quality public performance.

The third wave, which this book signifies, is *demonstration*. It reminds me of the generation I've met through the Young Leader Network (www.youngleader.org). Christianity in this context is more pastoral and more hands-on. Community is one of its primary values, but it's not tied to a building. Authenticity is its other primary value as it's more open and spontaneous than most other ways of doing church. It's more like a relationship over time, with a lot of involvement by the Holy Spirit. Like E-mail and the Internet, it's democratic and one-on-one. It's an anywhere and anytime connection.

Ginghamsburg personifies a very frontal, straight-at-you form of Christianity. It's an individual congregation very much in the vanguard of the third wave, through the spirit of one very passionate, engaged human being.

Three Experts: Fogel, Schaller, Drucker

I'm not alone seeing a shift of major proportions now happening in American religion. A *Wall Street Journal* (January 9, 1996) editorial by Robert Fogel is titled "The Fourth Great Awakening." This Nobel laureate professor of economics at the University of Chicago sees two major developments. First he says, "The new religious revival is fueled by a revulsion with the corruptions of contemporary society. It is a rebellion against preoccupation with material acquisition and sexual debauchery, against indulgence . . . and gluttony and financial greed . . . that titillate the senses and destroy the soul." Second, Fogel observes that "only the enthusiastic religions" have shown rapid growth, as characterized by spiritual intensity linked to conversion: "The upsurge in religiosity is seen . . . in an intensification of religious beliefs and in the mobilization of believers." *Real Followers* illustrates all these values.

Lyle Schaller knows more about American Christianity than anyone living. Schaller thoroughly agrees with Fogel that we're in the midst of a Fourth Great Awakening.

On the final page of Schaller's 1999 release, *Discontinuity and Hope* (Abingdon Press, page 226), he reviews American Christianity from the vantage point of the year 2050. He predicts that we will find, among other things: "The proportion of churchgoers in American Christianity who are deeply committed disciples and apostles will be at least double or triple the proportions of 1999, while the proportion of those who are 'lukewarm' in their faith will shrink dramatically." Further, "the proportion of Protestant congregations that accept the role as 'Kingdom-building churches' will at least quadruple, while the proportion that are driven by institutional survival goals will drop by at least one-half. That will be accompanied by an increase in the proportion that are implementing effective strategies for 'congregation building.' "

Pastors like Michael Slaughter are leading the way as they develop committed disciples in Kingdom-building congregations. They're on the front edge of something big and important that both Schaller and Fogel identify.

Peter Drucker is the social observer for the twentieth century that Alexis de Tocqueville was for the nineteenth century. Born in 1909, he immigrated from Europe to the U.S., first living in the New York City suburb of Bronxville, N.Y. Six years later, in 1962, when he sold his house to move to Vermont, the realtor asked him for the house keys. The Druckers couldn't find any keys because they had never locked their door.

At the time of the move, Peter told me, "We were a healthy society resting on a sick economy. Today we are a sick society resting on a healthy economy." How are churches changing to respond to these social needs? Drucker wrote in *Forbes* (October 5, 1998) that large churches "that have been growing so very fast in the U.S. since 1980 . . . are surely the most important social phenomenon in American society in the last 30 years."

Drucker calls the large-church movement, of which Ginghamsburg is such a good example, the most important *social* movement in the U.S. at present. His scope is not just religious; it covers the whole of American culture. Now that's worth betting your life on!

Real Passion, Real Conviction

You'll look in vain to hear Michael Slaughter say, "Let's *not* get all worked up about Jesus." To me Slaughter plays religion the way Michael Jordan played basketball in the NBA finals: with passion and intensity. He's not only worked up, he's sold out!

It's the same type of passionate commitment that Mother Teresa brought to the poor, and Martin Luther King brought to the Civil Rights movement. Michael

Slaughter brings the risk-taking attitude and intensity needed by today's church. Those are all people of intense passion who command a lot of authority, and appropriately so. They go about their calling with reckless abandon and ardor.

It's the way Winston Churchill felt when he was leading Britain against Hitler. It's the opposite of stoic, cynical, cerebral, and distant. This book is part of a big movement, and it shows you a way to get in touch with the can-do spirit that is propelling Third Wave American Christianity forward.

This is also a very demanding book. It's about keeping your appetites in control. It's very up-close and personal in asking about your religious ideals. It tells you to get real about your faith. It shows you how Christianity is counter-culture. It doesn't encourage you to look at religion from a safe vantage point. Instead, it calls you to engagement. This is a new spirit. It is not "business as usual" or "more of the same."

Real Followers tells me there is a new way where we, the "normal" people, are the carriers of religious life to others. Each of us is responsible ultimately to our Creator for being the carriers of Christ to others. We can't delegate that to the clergy. *Real Followers* won't let us remain what Michael Slaughter calls "priest dependent."

Power rips through the pages of this book. It gives me a deep sense that this movement is really happening. It contains a beguiling sense of risk and adventure, a willingness to act that draws me on. I can't hold my religious convictions at arm's length anymore.

Final Examination

My vision of life is that we'd all be well advised to practice one of Stephen Covey's well-known "seven habits": to begin with the end in mind. For the Christian, that's the time when each of us will stand before our Creator.

As I visualize that experience for myself, I believe there will be a final examination that consists of two questions. First, "What did you do about Jesus—did you accept God's offer or turn your back?" Second, "What did you do with what I gave you to work with? Not what I gave Mother Teresa, Martin Luther King, or Billy Graham, but *you.*"

This book is a great place to prepare people for the final exam. Everyone likes to learn the questions before the test takes place. If those are the questions, then this book is going to be very helpful to those who read it.

Bob Buford
Founder and Chairman, FaithWorks
   (www.faithworks.net)
Founder and Chairman, Leadership Network
   (www.leadnet.org)
Author, *Half Time* and *Game Plan*
Dallas, Texas

Chapter One

Invitation to a Journey: How God's Community Changed One Life

Do you want to be part of a God movement? You need to be challenged to take God at face value. But you can't make this journey alone. You need the camaraderie of a faith community that is significantly engaged in contemporary culture but not sold out to it. You will find help from a radical community of real followers who get honest with God.

C arolyn and I had a big argument during our second week of marriage. Our brief honeymoon on the East Coast was great. We had been married in late August, and when we got back to Ohio, I immediately had to begin my final year of college.

During that fateful first week of the fall semester, I left in the morning for school. Then in the afternoon I went directly from campus to meet with a church youth group I was leading.

When I walked into our apartment, it was about 7:00 P.M. There was Carolyn, standing in the hallway, projecting lots of negative energy. "Where have you been?" she asked. "I made a nice dinner for us." While I searched for just that right word (which never came), she continued, "You didn't even call."

Uh oh. No one had ever before asked me to call like that. I had never needed to.

"What have I done?" I asked myself. For the first time, I

realized that marriage means that I'm not my own anymore.

I carried on a brief dialogue in my mind: "I can't live the way I used to live. I'm only twenty-one years old and I've said I'll remain in this relationship for life. That could be a *very* long time! Do I really want this?"

My answer back was, "Yes." I knew that to have a good marriage, I'd have to change. I would have to learn responses based on commitment, not on feelings.

Community with God

Marriage is a lot like a relationship with God. When I said, "I do," to Carolyn, I pledged to be monogamous—to commit to one person for life. Likewise, becoming a Christian means to give up all gods but one. It means to have a personal faith-based relationship with this God through Jesus Christ.

Shortly after that argument, I remember attending a psychology class as part of my schoolwork. I and another student in the class were to sit in a dark, quiet room and observe counseling sessions through a one-way glass. There I was, in a cozy corner for long hours with an attractive woman who smelled good. As a newlywed I was surprised at my feelings, because I figured that God had cut the temptation nerve now that I was married.

It is not natural for a marriage to grow and thrive. We have passions inside that tempt us to do things that aren't healthy. That's why I need Christ to help me and transform me.

Sin is the breakdown in my relationship with God. It changes me from being like God to being on my own.

In the same way, it's not easy to be committed to one God for life. I have several gods each week. Self-sufficiency, envy, anger, rage, and indifference would rather rule me, to name a few. Sin is the breakdown in my relationship with God. It changes me from being like God to being on my own.

God's solution comes in two words that Jesus spoke during the first days of his ministry: "Follow me." (For example, see John 1:43.) He issued the "Follow me" call throughout his ministry on

"Follow me" . . . is the crux of Christianity. . . . If I'm a follower of Jesus Christ, then I've left everything to follow him.

earth. (See John 8:12; 10:27; 12:26; 13:36.) Then when Jesus rose from the grave he continued to say, "Follow me." (See John 21:19.) That is the crux of Christianity. Not "let's do lunch." Not "please form a social club."

The name "Christian" has been terribly cheapened and degraded. If I'm a follower of Jesus Christ, then I've left everything to follow him. I'm someone who maintains the mind-set of a servant. I'm someone who looks for community with God and with God's people.

The Central Idea of This Book

The underlying theme of this book asks what it means to be a real follower of Jesus. Just how many people do you know who are truly following him? Many inquire about Jesus, study about Jesus, and even "believe" in Jesus, but how many people are genuinely following Jesus?

The rest of this book explores this issue, but here's the short answer: Real followers go a different direction from the mainstream of our culture. The clear call of Jesus is this: "If any want to become my followers,

Real followers go a different direction from the mainstream of our culture.

ers, let them deny themselves and take up their cross daily and follow me. For those who want to save their life will lose it, and those who lose their life for my sake will save it" (Luke 9:23-24).

Today's "ladder life" is about acquiring, reaching, and attaining.

In contrast to taking up a cross, most Christians seem to be scaling a ladder, as we'll talk about later. Throughout our lives, our culture teaches us to be ladder climbers. In order to get to the top, we're told, we need to achieve certain goals. Our success is measured by the kind of house we own, the car we drive, and the people we know. Today's "ladder life" is about acquiring, reaching, and attaining.

For many of us, meeting Jesus doesn't change our prior stereotypes of what Christianity is all about. We bring Jesus into our world of ladder climbing, and ask him to help us in our ascent. We look to him to attain goals that center around comfort and security. It's almost as if we serve the "plastic" Jesus described in this song by an anonymous poet. The song is growing longer as it moves across the Internet:

> I don't care if it rains or freezes
> Long as I have my plastic Jesus
> Riding on the dashboard of my car.
> I can go 90 miles per hour
> Long as I have that plastic power
> Riding on the dashboard of my car.
> —Anonymous

The mandates of denial and giving up usually don't fit into our plan. Yet the Kingdom is not about ladders; it is about crosses. Jesus' message is that you don't find life in ascending; you find it in serving. Life is not saving and securing; instead, life comes from giving up. Life is not about success; life is about significance.

How My Journey Began

Each year, when we celebrate Christmas, I'm reminded that God comes to everyday people in ordinary, hard-to-find places like Tipp City, Ohio, population 6,000. God seems to delight in showing up around third-shift workers, like the shepherds of old who were working the graveyard shift. The angel chose to appear to them, and not to the politicians, celebrities, and superstars of Caesar's palace.

I know God still uses commonplace people, because he spoke to someone like me. I'm the kind of person who couldn't even successfully make it through a third year of high school math.

I grew up in a strong German Catholic neighborhood in Cincinnati, Ohio, and was raised within a mainline, traditional church setting. Most days, the last thing in the world I ever wanted to do was go to church. The last place I wanted to be was around religious people.

During my teenage years I found the church to be especially irrelevant to my interests and needs. I had gone to church enough to realize that it had the greatest message in the world. Yet church was the most boring experience I had in life.

Even when I had all but forgotten about God, he loved me with a love that

I know that God still uses commonplace people, because he spoke to someone like me.

refused (and still refuses) to let me go. That love showed up through God's people. My second grade Sunday school teacher told me: "Michael, God has created you with a purpose." My sixth grade public school teacher, a follower of Jesus, took me under his wing, almost like a son. He kept reaching out to me long after I graduated from his class.

My search for truth began in earnest at age nineteen during a particularly turbulent time. I was on a fast track to hell. My best friend would die years later at the age of thirty-one of a drug overdose, his body worn out from abusive living. Could I have been headed down the same path?

God loved me with a love that refused (and still refuses) to let me go.

I was about to flunk out of high school. I was also in a rock group that broke up when two members of the band were arrested for drug possession. In the midst of all that chaos, I had my first encounter with Jesus Christ.

In the coming years Jesus Christ became very real to me. During that time, something inside of me knew God was implanting an idea that said: "I've got a message for you, a mission for you. You're going to share my good news in a way that makes sense to everyday people. I want to use you to reach persons who suffer through the mundane, ordinary worlds of boring jobs, routine marriages, unexciting relationships, mediocre dreams, uneventful places, and even dull churches." I knew God wanted to use me to help people experience Jesus right where they are—on the job, at home, in marriage, and around their community.

When I am asked, "What do I hope people will remember me for?" My answer is: "That my life was a demonstration of a life lived in Jesus' hand, a demonstration of what God can do with the ordinary."

To this day my mission is to connect people to their God destiny. I have given myself—whatever days, months, or years I have left—to live the destiny God created me for and to help others discover and yield to their future.

Why Community Isn't Optional

My personal renewal is only half the equation, however. Beginning with my late teenage years, I've come to understand to whom I belong. When I went to college, I discovered a model of discipleship that closely paralleled the radical, faith-based community found in the book of Acts.

Through a campus Christian group, I learned that Christ's followers do their work in community. "I give you a new commandment, that you love one another. Just as I have loved you, you also should love one another. By this everyone will know that you are my disciples, if you have love for one another" (John 13:34-35). Lone Ranger Christianity will never be used by God to turn the world right-side up.

Lone Ranger Christianity will never be used by God to turn the world right-side up.

During this era, I also began to be influenced by Tom Skinner's book, *Black and Free,* and Howard Snyder's *The Problem of Wineskins.* Both writers stretched my imagination about what a church could become as people became transformed followers of Jesus Christ.

Then I was appointed to a committee-based congregation located in a town called Ginghamsburg, which had fewer than twenty houses. Our worship services were as lifeless and predictable as a mathematical formula. The church had formed in the 1800s when fourteen people made the commitment to be authentic Christ followers during a revival. In 1979, when Carolyn and I arrived, much of the church's spiritual vitality had been replaced by a small-minded focus on itself and on its comfortable traditions.

Although I had never seen or experienced radical discipleship in a church, I at least knew what it would probably look like. So Carolyn and I opened our home to a Wednesday night Bible study. We began building a group marked by a biblical sense of community.

I jokingly called the process "sanctified Amway" because of how devoted people became to our product— a life-changing relationship with Jesus Christ. I foresaw the leaders who emerged from our small-group community becoming the Joshuas and Deborahs of tomorrow's church. I had read stories of Fidel Castro overthrowing Cuba by training twenty or so revolutionaries. I knew that God could do the same with a church through the power of the gospel, even if we started with some pockets of rather frigid air.

John Ward (see sidebar) is one of those "revolutionary" people. He has often reminded us that from Ginghamsburg's inception, when a circuit rider proclaimed that the small prayer group from Ginghamsburg would one day have "impact on the world" from that place, God had a plan, which perhaps only now is fully unfolding. John has described many events surrounding our first years there, concluding that "it was the very hand of God who positioned a number of people, including Mike, to accomplish the work he intended to accomplish here."

> *True followers of Jesus are never going to belong to the majority. . . . Instead, we will always be a part of the minority.*

As that small, committed group of disciples grew and matured and became more visible in our community, I've needed to remember that true followers of Jesus are never going to belong to the majority on this earth. Instead, we will always be a part of the minority.

Wherever Jesus taught he drew three kinds of people: the curious, the convinced, and the committed. The largest sec-

John Ward: A Real Follower Who Sees People with Jesus' Eyes

I grew up in church. As a youth, I made a commitment to Christ. I remember doing Bible study in the woods at a church youth retreat. I got lost in Scripture. God was really touching me.

We came to Ginghamsburg Church a couple of months after Michael Slaughter did. I was invited by a friend, we came, and we became part of the first home Bible study training at the Slaughters. A book that got me off the fence was *Disciple* by Juan Carlos Ortiz. It showed God's desired relationship with me and what commitment to him really means.

The most radical change in the way I follow Jesus took place when I realized the Holy Spirit is inside me and that God intends to use me for his work. That understanding moved me from belief to empowerment. It marked a time of recommitment in my relationship with Jesus. A new level of relationship developed where I asked God to do what he wants in my life, not what I want.

God has gifted me in teaching and knowledge. He gives me insight into where people are, and then an ability to speak God's word to that need. Whether I teach, lead, or serve in ministry, the common thread is one of being used to equip other people, and to apply God's Word to those relationships.

I now see people with different eyes—as Jesus sees them, with all the potential he put in them, and with the desire to encourage them to fulfill that potential.

tion was the curious. They heard about this miracle worker and the fact that he did some rather exciting feats. They wanted to come out and see what all the excitement was about. The second-largest section was the convinced. These people believed that Jesus was the Son of God, but believing in Jesus does not always mean that you are committed to him. The third section was the committed. They had gone past the point of no return. They jumped. They took the leap of faith. For them, there was no more going back.

> *The committed . . . had gone past the point of no return. . . . They took the leap of faith. . . . Real followers believe they can fly.*

God did just that with the tiny band of people known as Ginghamsburg Church. Soon enough we began to develop a new mutual kingdom-of-God mind-set. We discovered that real followers believe we can fly in the sense that nothing holds us back. To be in Christ means to begin erasing all our self-imposed shortcomings, what we feel about ourselves, our inadequacies, our handicaps, our lack of formal education, our lack of religious background. As real followers we can begin to soar higher than we previously thought possible.

Our Marriage Is Like Walking with Jesus

Carolyn and I struggled with our marriage for years. We seriously contemplated whether we should divorce.

On June 1, 1992, our marriage totally turned around. On that date we both made a decision of unconditional commitment, no turning back, for better or worse, until death do us part. Although our marriage ceremony was almost twenty years earlier, my unconditional commitment did not occur until June 1, 1992.

In like manner, a lot of people believe in Jesus. We call it a commitment because we believe an intellectual truth or because we have committed ourselves to an intellectual idea.

However, commitment is more than a mental judgment. It goes beyond emotion or feelings. Sometimes people believe that because they "felt" something during worship, then God must have been there. Yet feelings change; deep, durable commitment is an act of the will.

Community Requires Commitment

This book is not only a call to that kind of radical commitment, but it's also about a commitment in community. Christianity is about the restoration of community. "Where two or three are gathered in my name, I am there among them," says Jesus (Matt. 18:20).

The movement of Christ is a movement of reconciliation. When sin came into the world, bringing brokenness, it destroyed community. Cain said about his brother Abel, "Hey, I'm not my brother's keeper." Wrong! Likewise, the human race keeps evolving into a culture of rugged individualists. White people have tried to rule over black people. Men have tried to rule over women. The rich have withheld power from the poor.

The movement of Christ is a movement of reconciliation.

When I watch religious television, I usually want to puke. So much of what masquerades as Christianity is a self-absorbed, personal spirituality.

Instead, Jesus spoke continually of a new kingdom that God is putting together. When Jesus talked about the church, he didn't use the language of an institution or a club where the measure of faithfulness is attendance or per-

Being a part of the body of Christ is not about attending, but about connection. It's not even about believing in Jesus, so much as being in Jesus.

formance. Instead he spoke of the church as a body—his body.

Fingers don't walk around by themselves. Toenails that are detached die. Being a part of the body of Christ is not about attending, but about connection. It's not even about *believing* in Jesus, so much as *being* in Jesus.

When the Spirit of God invaded the earth, all the believers were together in one place. In the following description of the first followers, notice how many times the → word *together* is stated or implied. "All who believed were together and had all things in common; they would sell their possessions and goods and distribute the proceeds to all,

> *I can't be connected to Christ if I'm not connected to Christ's people.*

as any had need. Day by day, as they spent much time together in the temple, they broke bread at home and ate their food with glad and generous hearts" (Acts 2:44-46).

In that quote, I found at least five times that the message is implied: "Following Jesus is about being together in community." What makes me a member of the Body is that I'm connected to Christ, and if I'm connected to Christ, I have to be connected to his people. I can't be connected to Christ if I'm not connected to Christ's people.

> *A lot of people—even religious people— . . . are militant . . . but they don't understand that their passion is for love.*

Jesus' Strategy Is Militant Love

Do you know that Jesus' strategy is to change the world through you and me? How will God do this? Through a militant love. There are a lot of people—even religious people—who are militant, but they don't understand that their passion is for love.

Some Christians think it is God's will to do acts of hate against other human beings. No! How will people know that we are the followers of Jesus? According to Jesus, the evidence is in how real followers love one another. (See John 13:34-35 quoted on page 27.) That's the test.

We are not called to be a chorus of judgment. We are called to be a counterculture community that demonstrates the love of God on planet Earth.

When people receive the gift of the Holy Spirit, God invades human life. The Holy Spirit is what enables real followers to go a different direction than the rest of our culture. A divine transformation is also what leads real followers to believe that they can change the world.

The Holy Spirit is what enables real followers to go a different direction than the rest of our culture.

Jesus has connected us to God's legacy. We have discovered that it's not our day job that really matters. Our real job is to fulfill the purpose for which God created us. Jesus said, "Let your light shine before others, so that they may see your good works and give glory to your Father in heaven" (Matt. 5:16).

Preparing for Real Discipleship

This book invites you to reaffirm what it is like to be a real follower of Jesus—both individually and in community. By the time you or your group finish these pages, you could have this confidence in God: As real followers of Jesus, we are going in a different direction than our culture. We believe we can "fly" through the Holy Spirit and we know that God, in us and through our church, will change the world.

As you begin this journey, would you consider pausing to voice the following prayer from your heart, either individually or with your small group?

> *Lord, I [we] want to be a real follower of Jesus under your command.*
> *I will no longer be my own. I will give myself up to you in all areas.*
> *Lord, make me all that you can. I put myself fully into your hands.*
> *Put me to doing, put me to suffering.*
> *Let me be employed for you or laid aside for you.*
> *Let me be full, let me be empty.*
> *Let me have all things, let me have nothing.*
> *I freely and with a willing heart give all to your pleasure and disposal. Amen.*

Discussion Questions

NOTE: Each chapter will contain group-based questions like this, also workable for individual reflection and journaling.

1. *Were you able to pray the prayer printed above? Which line made you most uncomfortable? Why?*

2. *This chapter summarized the book in one sentence: "Real followers go a different direction from the mainstream of our culture." What do you think Michael Slaughter means? In what ways does your current spiritual life go a different direction from your surrounding culture? What areas do you wish went a different direction?*

3. *Is your church known as a church where people have an extreme commitment to serving and having impact on the world? To what extent would you like to be involved with a church like this? How does your role at your own church make that sentence true for you? Please explain.*

4. *If you're meeting in a group, ask how you can pray for one another. Pray together.*

Joining the Movement

 Note to readers: Using this "Joining the Movement" headline, each chapter will also contain a suggestion suitable for a church-wide context, designed for peer reinforcement.

What could your entire church do to challenge and change the culture around you? Work hard to think "outside the box" here!

Example: What group could read this book together with you? If you're not a part of a home group, Sunday school class, worship team, or church board reading this book, how about recruiting a handful of friends? The commitment is simple: the next time you get together, you talk about the next chapter that each of you has read. You'll find questions like these at the end of each chapter.

Example: What would a "home run" look like the next step of your walk with God? That is, if God could use this book to take you to the next level spiritually, what would that be? Write down a specific dream, and date it. Show it to a friend or the group with whom you're reading this book. Plan to look back at what you wrote when you complete the final chapter.

Chapter Two

God Speaks Today—
Are You Listening?

God still speaks today. In fact, God is speaking now.
When God moves, are you willing to move? When
God stops, are you willing to stop? Are you ready?

When our oldest child, Kristen, went to college, we found ourselves looking with misty eyes at her photos on the various walls of our home. We mused over various plaques and awards on her dresser, and we reread notes or cards she'd sent us. It was a highly emotional time for us. We missed her badly!

But eighteen years of memories were not enough for us. We needed to hear her voice again. We wanted to keep up with her life—what she was feeling, what she was doing. We valued her input on developments in our lives.

Healthy relationships have a "now" quality.

Soon enough, we developed a family ritual. Sunday became our special evening when she phoned us or we placed a call to her. Even if we had heard from her during the week, I looked forward to reconnecting with Kristen on Sunday night.

No amount of great memories, videos, diaries, and mementos could replace the importance of hearing her voice today. Why? Healthy relationships have a "now" quality. They require ongoing communication.

Relationship Is Now

The deepest, driving thirst of a human being is to have that same kind of "now" relationship with the living God. You may have precious and special spiritual memories of the past. You may even have seen miracles of God first-hand. You may have read God's important wisdom for living (in our Bible) backward and forward.

But according to no less authority than Jesus Christ, these are not enough. You need to hear God's voice now, today. Jesus told his followers, "I still have many things to say to you but you cannot bear them now" (John 16:12).

Their past experiences with Jesus were incomplete. Jesus had more to tell them. Something was yet to come. Even if the story of Jesus were to be written (which it was in the Gospels), it would not include everything Jesus wanted them to hear.

What was missing? "When the Spirit of truth comes, he will guide you into all the truth; for he will not speak on his own, but will speak whatever he hears, and he will declare to you the things that are to come" (John 16:13).

To be a real follower, you need to ask yourself if you're ready for God to speak to you today.

What an incredible concept! God is present now. God the Holy Spirit will be there to teach you what you need to know next. This idea underscores the "now" quality of our relationship with God.

Do you want to strengthen your relationship with God? Would you like to discover all you are meant to be? To be a real follower, you need to ask yourself if you're ready for God to speak to you today. If so, three pathways will help you know how to respond.

1. Take Notice of How God Is Speaking

God spoke in ages past, and in a different way is speaking today. Jesus wouldn't tell us everything we need to know, so the Holy Spirit will speak to us today. The Spirit sets in perfect balance the historical (the written word) with the ongoing (the living word). We cannot limit the voice of God to one or the other alone.

Written Word

I still have Carolyn's love letters from before we got married. Our children found them at my mother's home, read them, and embarrassed me. It's important to have reminders of promises that have been made. They're essential foundations.

Do you ever keep letters from significant people in the past? Pictures from when your kids were little? Things a nephew or niece drew for you at school? If you're like most people, you do. Why? Because they are important reminders.

God's people also have a series of reminders. "Long ago God spoke to our ancestors in many and various ways by the prophets, but in these last days he has spoken to us by a Son, whom he appointed heir of all things, through whom he also created the worlds" (Heb. 1:1-2).

Thousands of years ago, God spoke to Moses. Moses chiseled God's commandments in stone, and the leaders of Israel kept the law for present and future generations. Later God spoke to the prophets. They put pen to parchment. They kept it, brought it out periodically, and remembered it.

In the time of Jesus, God spoke to Matthew, Mark, Luke, and John, and they wrote it down and preserved it. The same process was at work with the apostles.

All Scripture is God-breathed, and through it we can experience the pulse of God, the heart of God.

By the time the last apostle died, the church had many great written memories of God's promises, actions, and expectations. Those sixty-six books make up today's Bible, which is also known as the written Word of God. The Bible is God's diary. All Scripture is God-breathed, and through it we can experience the pulse of God, the heart of God.

At one point Jesus was in the wilderness being tempted by Satan. The devil took Jesus up to a high mountain and

Life outside the Word is narrow and limiting. The whole world is limited compared to the written Word of God.

showed him all the kingdoms, all the wealth, and all the power of the world. He told Jesus he would give it all to him if Jesus would break his relationship with God.

Through the whole temptation, Jesus quotes the written Word of God.

He keeps saying, "It is written, it is written, it is written." (See Matthew 4.) Jesus knew that life outside the Word is narrow and limiting. The whole world is limited compared to the written Word of God.

When I read the Bible, I can look at life through the eyes of Jesus. When I get stuck, if I look through the eyes of Jesus, then my fear turns to fearlessness. When I begin to throw a pity party for myself, if I look at my problem through the eyes of Jesus and I learn that nothing is impossible with God. I can do all things through Christ who strengthens me. When I look at people through the eyes of Jesus, the selfishness and self-focus in me changes to compassion.

I watched a preacher on television, Shaking his Bible, he stated, "You have absolute truth." His attitude scared me. I'm too limited to comprehend absolute truth. I'd rather ask, "Does absolute truth possess me?" If it does, then I won't be able to stop at quoting verses. Instead, I'll love my wife as Christ loved the church and gave himself for us. You can tell if you are possessed by truth, because your measure won't be how much Scripture you know, but how you treat other people because of how the Spirit has used Scripture to change your heart.

Shaking his Bible, he stated, "You have absolute truth."

. . .

I'd rather ask, "Does absolute truth possess me?"

When all is said and done, Jesus said, the outside of our lives will reflect what has happened inside of us. "I was hungry and you gave me food, I was thirsty and you gave me something to drink, I was a stranger and you welcomed me, I was naked and you gave me clothing, I was sick and you took care of me, I was in prison and you visited me" (Matt. 25:35-36).

If you're serious about being a real follower, it's pretty basic. If you have two coats, you'll give one to someone who has none.

If you're serious about being a real follower, it's pretty basic. If you have two coats, you'll give one to someone who has none. That's how you can tell if you're possessed with absolute truth.

But, despite the wonder and power of the Holy Book, you can't live off the written word alone. God also designed a way to keep the "now" quality of our relationship fresh and alive.

Living Word

Today God is speaking in an additional way. God continues to communicate to us through his Son. When Jesus was going away, he didn't say, "People, I'm going to heaven now, so I'll be leaving you a book." Or, "I'm going to leave you a list of rules." Or, "I'll be sending you instructions on a new way to design your houses of worship."

Instead, in one of his last recorded sayings, Jesus announced: "I am with you always, to the end of the age" (Matt. 28:20). So the new covenant is not a written work. Jesus' new covenant is a living relationship right now that is fresh every day.

God's book is a menu to tell you what is available, but Jesus is the food.

Jesus underscored this idea when we talked to the religious leaders of his day, "You keep talking about your God as the God of Abraham, Isaac, and Jacob," he said. In Jesus' time, these great heroes of faith had been dead for two thousand years. "You keep saying you follow the God of Abraham, Isaac, and Jacob. Don't you realize that God is also the God of the living and not just the God of the dead?" (paraphrase of Matt. 22:31-32).

The living word is different from the written word. Suppose you go to a restaurant. "Here's a menu," the host says. You open it and discover all kinds of great choices to make. You see the appetizers, the salads and soups, the entrees, and the desserts. But you don't pay for reading the menu. You pay if you eat the food. The menu is there to tell you what's available.

God's book is a menu to tell you what is available, but Jesus is the food—he even calls himself the "living bread" (John 6:51).

Jesus doesn't want you to be content with two-thousand-year-old letters, as inspired and meaningful as they are. God is speaking today as well. You can never completely know your unique purpose if you can't hear God speak today. Only by learning to listen to the Holy Spirit can you fulfill your deepest driving thirst to have a relationship with the living God and to fulfill your created purpose.

What happens when God speaks? The creation of the world began with the sound of God's voice, when God said, "Let there be light" (Gen. 1:3). God spoke and light appeared. God spoke the whole world into being.

Don't limit God's work in your life by having an imbalanced relationship between God and yourself.

That principle works the same today. As God speaks, it sets free the creative process in you and me. Don't limit God's work in your life by having an imbalanced relationship between God and yourself.

2. Make Sure You Are Listening

I remember a time when our son, Jonathan, had just started one of his high school baseball seasons. He'd been through four games already. He was a little discouraged because he had entered a batting slump—and hitting is what he does best!

Jonathan was frustrated. He kept remembering every-thing his coaches had said over previous years of train-ing, but he couldn't figure out what he was doing wrong. He needed a new word.

Then he played against another high school team whose coach had been his summer baseball coach. Of his three times at bat, Jonathan walked once and struck out twice. When we got home that night, there was a message on our answering machine from the summer coach. "Jonathan," he said. "Call me. I saw something in your hands today that's causing you to mess up. You're hold-ing your hands below your letters. You've got to get your hands higher."

The coach gave feedback to Jonathan the day Jonathan made the errors. "Raise the bat," the coach advised. That's what Jonathan did, and at his next game he hit a home run.

Tuning In Today

A coach gives feedback on what someone is doing today. The coach sees things we can't see. A coach meets us where we are at present.

Our job is to make sure we're listening.

Am I listening to the voice of the Holy Spirit with that same eagerness that Jonathan experienced when he heard that phone message from his coach? One of the writers of the Bible says, "About this we have much to say that is hard to explain, since you have become dull in understanding" (Heb. 5:11). In essence, God says to us as children, "I have much to tell you, so much more, but you have developed this bad habit of not listening."

Hold on, you might be thinking, *am I not reading this book? And do I not usually stay awake at church? Doesn't that count?* No, that's not the same as listening to what God is saying. You are studying concepts. Churches and Christians have become concept-centered. We study what God said to Moses; we study what God said to the psalm writer; we study what Jesus said to his disciples; we study what Paul said to the church. Because we have become concept-centered by studying principles, we are not Christ-centered and Holy Spirit-centered. We're missing what God is saying to us today.

Christ's followers are called children of God because they're able to hear and follow their parent's voice. The Bible says, "For all who are led *Children of God keep tuning into God's voice in the present.* by the Spirit of God are children of God" (Rom. 8:14). Paul doesn't say that what identifies "children of God" is how well they have memorized two-thousand-year-old letters. Nor are they those who understand the principles.

Instead, we're identified as children of God because today we're able to sense our parent's leading and respond to it. Children of God keep tuning into God's voice in the present.

Living Off Your Own Walk

Too many people today suffer from what I call the Samuel syndrome. As a boy, Samuel literally lived in "church" (a holy shrine in his day would be the equivalent of our church buildings). Even though he was there all the time, he wasn't able to hear God's voice. He was what I call "priest dependent." He counted on God to speak through his pastor. Like many people today, Samuel depended on the pastor's experience of God's voice. *Like many people today, Samuel depended on the pastor's experience of God's voice.*

As an intern in the church, Samuel was trained in how

to study God's word. He heard the pastor, he understood the principles, but he couldn't hear God's voice. He understood God's concepts, but he didn't really know the relational presence of the Lord.

One day God spoke to Samuel, but Samuel didn't know it was God. So he ran to the priest, Eli, and asked what was happening. Maybe Samuel had developed a bad habit of not being able to hear. Or maybe it was time to learn how. "Now Samuel did not yet know the LORD, and the word of the LORD had not yet been revealed to him" (1 Sam. 3:7).

God spoke to Samuel a second and third time, but Samuel still couldn't understand. Finally Eli told Samuel to return to his bed, not to write anything down in his notebook, and this time to say, "Speak, LORD, for your servant is listening" (1 Sam. 3:9 NIV).

How does that story translate to today? One application happens when you come to church. Don't look for a nice message from your pastor and yet miss the voice of God.

Here are some ways we hear God's voice today. These will help keep you from becoming "priest dependent." These will help you discover more of your created purpose.

Learning How to Hear

Sometimes God's voice comes through people. Usually I discount anyone who begins, "God told me to tell you. . . ." In my experience, that's usually a red flag from a control freak. Instead, I remember coming to church with a personal problem on my heart. A woman in our fellowship came up and said something to me. She didn't know the situation I was dealing with, and yet her words directly addressed my circumstances. I sensed that she was the instrument of God's voice. We need to discern God's voice when people speak.

Another way we hear God speak is in particular places.

Sometimes we're more receptive to hear God say something in a certain place. God told the prophet Jeremiah to go down to the potter's house. There was something about the atmosphere at the potter's house. In effect, God said, "Go down to the potter's house for I'm getting ready to say something to you there." (See Jeremiah 19:1.)

I began chatting with a woman and her daughter from the Dayton area who had never been in our building before. The woman said, "Something about this place is special. As soon as we walked into this building we could tell the Spirit was doing something unique here." I don't know why, but for many people it's true.

When you identify those times and places where God has spoken to you in the past, make sure you go to those places often. Intentionally put yourself in those situations.

Another way God will speak to us is through nature. Where did Moses hear God speak? From a bush! When you're out walking, look and listen. "The heavens are telling the glory of God; and the firmament proclaims his handiwork" (Ps. 19:1). God is constantly speaking.

Another way God speaks is through the inner voice. Inside of you there is something that's almost like a sixth sense. It's even beyond reason. Sometimes you know something is right or wrong. Jesus says, "My sheep hear my voice" (John 10:27). We learn to recognize it as we listen for it.

How do you know you're listening to the quiet promptings of God and not the anchovies on your pizza? One test of God's voice is that the result or consequence will always honor God. It would never disgrace or shame God. It will always build people in love. It will never slander or tear people down.

Another way God speaks is through the written Word. There is a consistency and a coherence between what God has said to Abraham and Sarah, to Mary and Joseph, and to what God will say to me. Some of God's commands are situational—like when Jesus told his disciples to get the Arabian donkey for Palm Sunday weekend. Yet I also find timeless principles in which God speaks in brand new ways for my situation.

Avoid "priest dependency" by:
•Listening to other people
•Going to special places
•Experiencing nature
•Recognizing the inner voice
•Searching the written Word

I make sure to go to this place every day.

However you recognize the ways that God deals with you, Jesus and his apostles taught that God is speaking today. The question is this: Are you "priest dependent," or are you listening? You can't live off someone else's experience; God wants to speak to you!

3. Move Ahead in Response

At the end of this chapter, you'll have an opportunity to write down what you think God is saying to you today. If you're afraid you might not have anything to write down, remember this: God speaks most clearly to those who are willing to do what God says. You want to hear God? Then determine right now that you will move ahead in response to what you are hearing.

God speaks most clearly to those who are willing to do what God says.

One of Christ's followers who heard regularly from God—through dreams, a quiet voice, and other means—was the apostle Paul. Why did God speak so clearly to him? Because Paul was willing to act and move on what he heard. Resistance is not the key to hearing God; obedience is. As Paul explained when he was telling about his conversion, "I was not disobedient to the heavenly vision" (Acts 26:19).

Jesus is the perfect model of ever moving ahead in response to how God the Father spoke to him. He said, "I do as the Father has commanded me" (John 14:31).

I Wasn't Willing

I recall a trip that I needed to make to a speaking engagement in Des Moines, Iowa, at a time when Des Moines had just received a huge snowstorm with up to 15-foot drifts. My starting point was the Dayton airport a few minutes from my home. I was tired and, frankly, I didn't want to go. When I got in line to check in at TWA, I saw a notice that the flight had been canceled. *Great!* I thought. *I get to go back home.*

As I waited in line, I looked at my ticket and saw that the first leg of my trip would take me to St. Louis, which I knew was also snowed in. I became even more convinced that I'd be sent home. *I get to go home,* I almost sang to myself.

After thirty minutes of these happy thoughts, it was finally my turn at the ticket counter. The agent burst my bubble by saying, "We can get you to Des Moines through another airline. It will take you through Cincinnati. You'll get in late tonight so you can speak tomorrow morning."

The Lesson of the Cloud

As I hung my head and made my way down to the other counter, I remembered the story in the book of Numbers when the children of Israel were out in the wilderness for forty years. During that era, God revealed himself by a cloud. They moved or pitched tent according to that cloud. "Whenever the cloud lifted from over the tent, then the Israelites would set out; and in the place where the cloud settled down, there the Israelites would camp" (Num. 9:17).

On my walk to the other counter, exhausted, I could hear those Jewish people following this cloud, "I'm tired. I'm exhausted. When is this going to end? Doesn't God know I'm tired? When is the cloud going to stop?" But the cloud kept moving, and so the people kept walking.

I imagined a sister and brother getting their second breath, just like I hoped would eventually come to me. Then, in my mind's eye, I saw the cloud stop. Why is it stopping? Can't God see that now they have enough energy to go on? They feel like moving. Just when they caught their second wind, the cloud stopped.

> **When God moves, we're willing to move. When God stops, we're willing to stop.**

God used that story to teach me a valuable lesson. The issue is not how we feel—whether we're tired or have energy. The point is that when God moves, we're willing to move. When God stops, we're willing to stop.

So, as I handed my ticket to the ticket agent, I said, "Okay, Lord, regardless of whether I am tired or rested, I will go when you go and I will stop when you stop."

Real followers say to God, "I am willing, regardless of whether I'm tired or rested, to keep going when you go, and to stop when you stop." We take seriously Jesus' teaching about the cross: "Then he said to them all, 'If any want to become my followers, let them deny themselves and take up their cross daily and follow me' " (Luke 9:23).

Application Project

With your group, or individually, please pray aloud this prayer. Let these be your words to God:

Speak, Lord, for your servant is listening. Regardless of whether I'm tired or rested, without careful calculation, I will go when you go, and I will stop when you stop. Amen.

Now, with that prayer in mind, search out what the voice of God is saying to you now. Write down your impressions:

• Perhaps God is calling you to "cast all your anxiety on him, because he cares for you" (1 Pet. 5:7).
• Perhaps there is a relationship that has been broken. "So when you are offering your gift at the altar, if you remember that your brother or sister has something against you, leave your gift there before the altar and go; first be reconciled to your brother or sister, and then come and offer your gift" (Matt. 5:23-24).
• Perhaps something is distracting you, keeping you from confidently sensing that "whether you eat or drink, or whatever you do, do everything for the glory of God" (1 Cor. 10:31).
• Perhaps God is inviting you to deeper intimacy through cultivating a passion for God's closeness.
• Or . . .

Now as you begin to take action, be sure to verbalize what you are hearing and learning to someone else.

Discussion Questions

1. Describe your personal feelings about dependence on the pastor or minister for discerning God's will. Do you agree that the Bible is like a menu? What other description might fit your perception of the Bible as a source for God's plan?

2. In what ways do the ideas of this chapter press you to greater faith?

> *3. If you recall a time when you sensed God speaking
> to you and you responded in obedience, would you
> be willing to tell the group about it? (Or to describe
> it in your journal?) As you look back, what was the
> greatest lesson you learned?*
>
> *4. If you're meeting in a group, ask how you can pray
> for one another. Pray together.*

Joining the Movement

 What could your entire church do to challenge
and change the culture around you?

Example: If you have a teaching ministry at church, meet
with other teachers to ask how your classes or groups
could be more conducive to hearing God speak. For
instance, when you plan your lessons, do you focus more
on information transfer or on obedient application? Try
starting your class by asking, "Last week we talked about
_____; what happened during recent days as you
responded to God in that area?" End your class or group
with an opportunity for response: "What has God said to
us today?" instead of "We'll pick it up here next week."

Example: If you're part of a team or small group at
church, would you be willing to introduce an experi-
ment? Describe the idea of improving your spiritual listening skills, and suggest that you designate the
upcoming week (or month) to encourage one another
in this area. Ask people to pair off together, each
promising to pray that the other will hear and respond
to God's living voice this next week and to talk together about what happened before the next time your
entire group or team meets. Then make time at your
next gathering to hear what happened!

Chapter Three

God—More Than a Preference

We seek safe gods—the kind who will bring us to a comfortable place, who will reduce risk and help us achieve our desired futures. There is a self-serving religion masquerading as Christianity, and it is cultural and counterfeit. You should check it out because you might be serving another god.

H ave you ever participated in a religious survey? The question about religion often uses the phrase, "What is your religious preference?"

In ancient times, the question would have been, "Who is your God?" At least that question is bold and direct and it invites a dignified answer. But the question, "What is your religious preference?" leads to an answer like, "Well, I like my coffee black, my wine white, my sex straight, my shirts medium-starched, and oh, yeah, my religious preference would be . . ."

Real followers see through these false representations. Real followers instead follow a road that most people don't travel. Real followers learn how to find God in the ordinary, everyday places of daily life.

Avoid a Cafeteria Spirituality

Many current movies and TV shows involve the supernatural. From *City of Angels* and *Touched by an Angel,* to

What Dreams May Come and *Seventh Heaven,* spirituality is a hot subject. Even in the book world, from Deepak Chopra's *Seven Spiritual Laws of Success* to Jerry Jenkins's Left Behind series, the topic of divinity is hugely popular right now as we enter a new millennium.

God has become a preference —an optional, leisure-time activity

Is this heightened spiritual interest good news for the church? With so many people interested in spiritual things, you would expect churches to be growing, right? Wrong. Churches across North America, especially mainline ones, continue to decline. In fact, today's developments represent the first spiritual awakening in American culture where the church is not on the leading edge.

Why are so many people discounting Christianity? One reason is that God has become a preference—an optional, leisure-time activity that has little to do with most people's perception of day-to-day life.

Many people who go by the name of Christian have adopted a cafeteria-type spirituality.

People today select a god as if they're choosing a car. We seek the kind of god who will bring us to a comfortable place, who will reduce risk and help us achieve our desired futures. We seek safe gods.

Many people who go by the name of Christian have adopted a cafeteria-type spirituality. It is cultural, counterfeit, and widely popular. This variation of the Jesus way is a religion masquerading as Christianity, and it might well lead you to serve another god.

The Weekend God

Some people, for example, serve a weekend god. What they do in church has no relationship to how they behave during the week. This "private religion" god is so widespread that when the real deal shows up, something seems wrong.

Many people serve a god who won't interfere in a person's daily routines. A widespread attitude is that what I do in private should be of no concern to God. If a more active god shows up, the follower gets identified as an extremist!

The Rabbit's Foot God

Other people have bought stock in a heavenly money-market adviser. Lots of radio and television preachers assure me that God's primary concern is my financial well-being. They say that God has promised to get me that loan for my new home. God can help me get a promotion. God wants to give me financial wealth so that I can be comforted by the material possessions of this world.

Who wouldn't like a God like that? Jesus becomes little more than a rabbit's foot.

The Master Magician God

For others, God is primarily a master magician. "Oh, Jesus, show us a sign. We've come to look at the power of the Holy Spirit being demonstrated," they pray. "Jesus, wow us as a magician would." People spend a lot of money traveling to churches in the hope of watching God do before-their-eyes supernatural miracles.

We've got to be careful to place more priority on the giver than on the gift, on getting beyond the fireworks to the fire underneath. Cafeteria-style religions present a Jesus who will support your own beliefs and lifestyles. In those cases, Jesus stays on a leash. Major parts of God's identity get checked at the office or bedroom door.

Serious Implications

Why do people write off Christianity in a time of increased spiritual hunger? Because too often it's hard to distinguish true followers of Jesus from those who are masquerading as Christians.

When God's Spirit comes into your life, you literally bear the presence of Christ everywhere you go.

At a baseball game, I began talking to a friend who told me about troubles he was having with his ex-wife, who happens to be a Christian. He said, "If this is what Christianity is about, I don't want to have anything to do with it."

That's what happens when we pick and choose religion from a cafeteria menu. Not only is it possible for us to fall for a different god, but we can confuse others who are honestly searching. Whether we like that or not, we are the only image some people have for Christianity. The track record of our life is all many people will experience and know about Christianity.

Jesus said . . . to "be my witnesses" is to be a Christ-bearer at the deepest roots of who I am, what I do, and where I go.

Charles Barkley, the NBA basketball star, once stated, "I don't want to be a role model." In reality, you are a role model, even if you don't think so or want to be. Everyone is. I once read that even the most introverted among us will influence 10,000 people in our lifetime. You are a role model whether you like it or not. The important question is, "What are you modeling?"

The word *Christian* means Christ-bearer. When God's

Spirit comes into your life, you literally bear the presence of Christ everywhere you go.

Jesus tells his followers, "You will receive power when the Holy Spirit has come upon you; and you will be my witnesses . . . to the ends of the earth" (Acts 1:8). Too many Christians have reduced the meaning of *witness* to the idea of information broker or truth speaker. Instead, to "be my witnesses" is to *be* a Christ-bearer at the deepest roots of who I am, what I do, and where I go.

Plan to Journey the Road Less Traveled

Jesus once met a man who showed all of the ingredients of success. He had health, wealth, and intelligence, but he felt incomplete. Something was missing. When he heard that Jesus was in the area, he "ran up and knelt before him, and asked him, 'Good Teacher, what must I do to inherit eternal life?' " (Mark 10:17). He asked Jesus in essence, "Where can I find life?" He was looking for a quality of life beyond that which he had experienced.

Jesus answered in terms his inquirer could understand: "You know the commandments: 'You shall not murder; You shall not commit adultery; You shall not steal; You shall not bear false witness; You shall not defraud; Honor your father and mother' " (Mark 10:19).

It May Challenge Your Pride

This rich inquirer seems to have reduced Christianity to a list of moral behaviors. He felt he knew the rules and had followed them. That's why he replied to Jesus, "Teacher, I have kept all these since my youth" (Mark 10:20).

He illustrates the danger of what happens when you reduce Christianity to a moralistic list of rules: it breeds pride. You think to yourself, "I'm a pretty good person. I'm surely better than some of the people I am around."

This kind of pride is the root of all sin. It's behind the

racism that led three white men in Texas to chain a black man to a truck and drag him until his body was not recognizable. When Serbians brutally massacre Albanians (or vice versa), more than ethnic hatred is present. At heart is a pride that says I am better than you. Those incidents aren't merely about morals or a lack of belief; they stem from lifestyles, priorities, and values.

As for the rich man, "Jesus, looking at him, loved him and said, 'You lack one thing; go, sell what you own, and give the money to the poor, and you will have treasure in heaven; then come, follow me' " (Mark 10:21).

Jesus' answer was probably not what his interviewer had predicted—or desired. Jesus' call certainly wouldn't have been confused as a recipe for success. In fact, this seeker might have decided that Jesus would take him a way he didn't want to go, for "when he heard this, he was shocked and went away grieving, for he had many possessions" (Mark 10:22).

It May Identify You with "Losers"

Why are seekers sometimes turned off to Jesus? From the world's perspective, it's easy to see Jesus as a loser.

From the world's perspective, it's easy to see Jesus as a loser.... Here is someone executed by the state ... and he says, "Follow me."

They might say he failed in his mission. Here is someone executed by the state for subversive activity and he says, "Follow me."

From our youth, most of us were taught that we need to network with the right people. But the people Jesus will hook me up with might be the sort excluded by country clubs, sororities, and fraternities. Jesus might link you with those whom the world sees as the wrong people. Their lack of worldly empowerment can make them seem like a fellowship of oddballs.

It May Be Uncomfortable or Unpopular

In addition, Jesus invites us to the way of discomfort. The advice he gave the rich ruler was typical of how Jesus challenged people's sense of security and ease. Another man came up to Jesus and told him, "I will follow you wherever you go." Jesus said that he should calculate the price, for "foxes have holes, and birds of the air have nests; but the Son of Man has nowhere to lay his head" (Luke 9:57-58).

Jesus calls his followers to a road that is less traveled. Jesus said the majority will choose the road that is wide and easy: "For the gate is wide and the road is easy that leads to destruction, and there are many who take it" (Matt. 7:13).

Jesus calls his followers to a road that is less traveled.

By contrast, the road that leads to life is narrow and less traveled. "For the gate is narrow and the road is hard that leads to life, and there are few who find it" (Matt. 7:14).

The Jesus road isn't a popular journey. Most people will not naturally want to go there. It requires a commitment to go against the crowd if necessary. It may lead us to bypass certain material comforts. It begins and ends in relationship, not in keeping rules.

It May Change Your Church

When the Holy Spirit invades people's lives, their church is radically changed. "Now the whole group of those who believed were of one heart and soul, and no one claimed private ownership of any possessions, but everything they owned was held in common" (Acts 4:32). They shared everything they had. "Great grace was upon them all. There was not a needy person among them" (Acts 4:33-34).

When the Holy Spirit invades people's lives, their church is radically changed.

A church that lives like this could be dangerous! You can tell a lot about a God by the behavior and the character of the follower. Maybe that's why "day by day the Lord added to their number those who were being saved" (Acts 2:47).

Are you ready to buy into that kind of lifestyle? Changes like that may start happening when you receive power as the Holy Spirit comes upon you to be Jesus' witness.

Look for God in the Ordinary

Moses, age eighty, had spent the last forty years in the Arabian desert, tending his father-in-law's sheep. One day, as he was leading the flock through the wilderness, he "came to Horeb, the mountain of God. There the angel of the LORD appeared to him in a flame of fire out of a bush; he looked, and the bush was blazing, yet it was not consumed" (Exod. 3:1-2).

Most of the time, God speaks and appears in very ordinary ways and in very ordinary places.

An angel from God appeared, but it did not look like an angel. Instead it had taken the form of a burning bush.

Most of the time, God speaks and appears in very ordinary ways and in very ordinary places. I often wonder how many people God appears to today, but they don't notice because they aren't watching for it.

"Then Moses said, 'I must turn aside and look at this great sight, and see why the bush is not burned up'" (Exod. 3:3). When Moses had come over, God called to him from within the bush. "Moses, Moses!" And Moses said, "Here I am" (v. 4).

Perhaps Moses was stale in his soul and perhaps he needed eyes to see. Perhaps he was simply unaware that the ground where he walked was not limited to ordinary soil. God had to say, "Come no closer! Remove the sandals from your feet, for the place on which you are standing is holy ground" (Exod. 3:5).

Many Christians miss similar God moments. We think today is just another ordinary day, framed in just another ordinary place. But where you are standing right now, in your condition, in this place, is holy ground because God is present. The current opportunities before you could represent the very gate of heaven. They can be the center of the activity of God.

Instead of believing that God is continually present and is continually seeking to communicate with us, we too often think of God as being "over there." God, we assume, is someplace other than where we are. As the Creator of the universe, God often appears in our imaginations in the throne room of heaven, or perhaps in big, ornate temples, or around stained glass and gilded crosses. Whatever your mental picture, it is probably something that looks very different from the ordinary place where you spend your days and evenings.

The truth is that God is a God who speaks through very common, ordinary ways. Even the name of God underscores this idea. When Moses asks what God's name is, "God said to Moses, 'I AM WHO I AM.' He said further, 'Thus you shall say to the Israelites, "I AM has sent me to you"'" (Exod. 3:14).

The name "I AM" means present tense, right here, with you always. It implies that we're standing in the middle of the activity of God, even if we haven't noticed. God seems to be telling Moses, "Go back and tell the people that they are standing in the middle of the door of heaven."

This idea matches many other ways that God has appeared. God spoke to Adam and Eve in the garden, to Mary and Joseph in a stable, to the early apostles in their jail cells. King Solomon, wisest man on earth, learned to see God's activity in his neighbor's unkempt backyard. According to Proverbs 24:30-32: "I passed by the field of one who was lazy . . . it was all overgrown with thorns. . . . Then I saw and considered it; I looked and received instruction."

When most of us walk by smelly trash cans, all we see is garbage. Solomon, however, realized God is a God of the ordinary and he asked, "What is God saying?" Right in the middle of his day, he realized that he was on holy ground.

Most of us see no more than the pile of work that is unfinished, the lawn that needs to be mowed, the child we are having trouble with. By not pausing to look below the surface for a spiritual insight, we forget that we are standing on holy ground, in the middle of the activity of God, and in the presence of God.

Many . . . have forgotten that their workplace . . . could be the door of heaven.

I am a Christian because of the person of Jesus Christ. Jesus is far more than the greatest teacher who ever lived. As Holy Week reminds us each year, he was crucified for claiming to be God. As he told one group of critics, "Before Abraham was [born], I am" (John 8:58).

In Moses' day, God, the great I AM, was continually in the midst of the children of Israel. Continuing that claim, Jesus is continually present with his church today. According to his last words on earth and the last sentence in the Gospel according to Matthew, "I am with you always" (Matt. 28:20). That means he is with you right now. Where you are, Jesus is constantly present. So when I look at Carolyn, I realize that she is a child of God and Jesus is present in her life. There is no room for boredom in marriage when I realize I am on holy ground. A lot of people look at their spouse and see nothing more than a husband or wife; they forget they might be on holy ground. Many people are bored in their job and can't wait to get to the weekend. They have forgotten that their workplace, no matter how ordinary, could be the door of heaven.

Barbara Bixler: A Real Follower at the Counseling Center

I try to do what Jesus wants me to do, and that means lending a hand wherever I can. By day I'm employed as a program director by a private organization that specializes in providing services and support to people who have developmental disabilities such as mental retardation. During the week, and occasionally on weekends, I often serve as a receptionist at the New Creation Counseling Center.

It's not even work. I'm communicating with people over the phone, helping determine who to hook them up with. I also meet whomever the Lord sends through the door. It might be someone who doesn't have an appointment but perhaps needs a listening ear. I love what I do.

To me, radical Christianity is being the hands and feet of Christ, ready to serve and give witness whenever and to whomever. Maybe that's why we're such a close-knit organization at the counseling center, as we reach out with the Spirit to serve others in Jesus' name.

This truth applies even at church. Two people can be at the same place and see two different things. Some go home saying, "We were in the presence of God! We heard the voice of God!" Others will leave and their biggest insight is, "The coffee was bitter this morning." That's why people like Barbara Bixler (see page 63) can find such fulfillment in what other people might consider to be the "ordinary."

You cannot go forward in your life . . . if you don't understand what it means to be standing in the middle of the activity and presence of God.

You cannot go forward in your life, nor can your church go forward in its mission, if you don't understand what it means to be standing in the middle of the activity and presence of God. It is essential that God's people remember what we are about.

That is why it is so important to look at your blooming flowers and uncut grass and moody teenager and say, "What is God saying?" Or when your boss comes in and reams you out, you need to ask the question, "What is God saying?" When God has your attention, you can discover what it is that you are about.

When God has your attention, you can discover what it is that you are about.

Even if you don't know how to see holy ground where you live and work, you can at least begin to figuratively take off your shoes. Ask God to help you see what you need to see, to hear what you need to hear, to respond in the way you need to respond. Begin to write down what you think God is showing you. Become part of a small group or class or team at church where you can tell others what you are learning. Take the next step of discipleship urged by your pastor. Meet God regularly through the stories and teachings of the Bible. Reach out to someone else, work against injustice, demonstrate compassion, and tell someone what a great God you serve. From presidents to stock clerks, we are on a mission, but it is not our mission; it is God's mission. That is why you were sent to planet Earth. It is not because you have something great to bring to the table. It is God who wants to show the world what he can do through you. If you remember where you are and you remember what you are about, you are never going to get stale in your journey with God.

Discussion Questions

1. *How comfortable are you with the idea of looking for spiritual insight in common, everyday events? How has God shown up recently in the mundane, ordinary routines of your life?*

2. *What fears do you have as you take the "road less traveled"?*

3. *In what ways have you yielded to a pick-and-choose Christianity? What pushed you to limit who God is?*

4. *If you're meeting in a group, ask how you can pray for one another. Pray together.*

Joining the Movement

 What could your entire church do to challenge and change the culture around you?

Example: Many of the quotations (enlarged bold text) in this book underscore the more radical challenges that real followers need to deal with. How could you publicize the ones that speak most to you or your group? Is there a door or wall at your church building where you could post one of the quotes? If you are involved in any of your church's printed communications, could you copy some of the quotations? (No publisher permission is needed to cite 100 words or less, as long as you indicate the source.)

Example: The second-to-the-final paragraph of this chapter (beginning "Even if you don't know," page 64) mentions almost a dozen ways that you can act upon what you are learning. Would any of these be a suitable project for one of the church's classes, teams, or groups where you are a member?

Chapter Four

God Created You
for a Unique Mission

We have been taught that life centers around self-focus: what I want, where I want to be, what I want to achieve, and what I want to have. That's the worldview of the predominant culture. But as you nurture God's thoughts and network with God's people, you will move in a direction counter to the rest of the culture because you will be surrendered to a God-focus.

D o you believe God created you for a unique mission? Jesus Christ wants his followers to do even greater things than he himself did when he was here on earth. Jesus, after rising from the dead and going up to heaven, sent the Holy Spirit to each of his followers. The Spirit empowers us to use our gifts and relationships, both individually and in community, to carry out God's mission.

What could be more important than a mission for God? If someone asked you to summarize the unique contribution that you, as one of almost six billion potential followers of Christ, are alone called by God to carry out in this world, what would you say? Could you ink it here in twenty-five words or less?

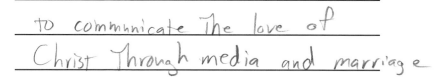

To communicate The love of Christ Through media and marriage

Real followers not only know the particulars of their distinctive mission, but each day they discover one more piece of how to live it out.

Nurture God's Thoughts

God's mission is easy to miss. If you or I are running ahead of God, we won't hear it or see it. It's possible to map out a day, a business agenda, or even a series of life goals without knowing God's thoughts and without the certainty of moving in God's presence.

> *God's mission is easy to miss if you or I are running ahead of God.*

That's why some of Jesus' first instructions after his resurrection mean: "Wait. Remain still until you're sure you're moving with God's plan. Hang on until you know you have God's presence, because this mission is impossible to do in your own strength or resources." (See Acts 1:3-14.)

Can You Think God's Thoughts?

As you then walk in step with God, you have a tremendous privilege. Jesus said that everyone who calls on the name of the Lord can begin to know the mind of God. Anyone—not just pastors or great saints or Bible scholars—can dream the thoughts of God.

According to prophecy, all kingdom people, regardless of gender, race, economic status, social status, or age, will have the ability to think God's thoughts for the purpose of acting on God's plan for the future. "In the last days it will be, God declares, that I will pour out my Spirit upon all flesh, and your sons and your daughters shall prophesy, and your young men shall see visions, and your old men shall dream dreams. Even upon my slaves, both men and women, in those days I will pour out my Spirit; and they shall prophesy" (Acts 2:17-18).

"The last days" describes the time window when anyone can have the fullness of God's presence. It refers to the era between Jesus' time and today. That means right now you can dream God's dreams and know God's thoughts so that you can be guided in how to direct your week.

Right now you can dream God's dreams and know God's thoughts so that you can be guided in how to direct your week.

How can God's Spirit be made available to you in that way? You begin by nurturing God's thoughts.

Most of us need to learn this nurturing process. God's thoughts are not obvious thoughts. Nor do they come naturally. Nor are they automatic. "Do not be conformed to this world, but be transformed by the renewing of your minds, so that you may discern what is the will of God— what is good and acceptable and perfect" (Rom. 12:2).

Some people develop inspiring visions for what their life potential could be, but few people have the sense of supernatural intervention that provides the ability to think God's thoughts today. "For my thoughts are not your thoughts, nor are your ways my ways, says the LORD" (Isa. 55:8).

Self-focus Conflicts with a God-focus

The discrepancy stems from two opposing attitudes. Over time God can transform stinking thinking into a lifestyle that nurtures God's thoughts.

First is the worldview of the predominant culture in which you and I have been raised. We have been taught that life centers around self-focus. According to this view, life is about what I want to do, where I want to be, what I want to achieve, and what I want to have. The center of the universe is "me."

We have been taught that life centers around self-focus . . . but . . . a person filled with the Holy Spirit puts the focus on knowing and pleasing God.

People led by the Spirit of God give their world to God. When you are led by the Spirit, your desires are to know and please God. Spirit-directed people gear their whole lifestyle and focus toward the purpose of God.

Four Keys to Success

How do we nurture God's thoughts? The first followers "devoted themselves to the apostles' teaching and fellowship, to the breaking of bread and the prayers" (Acts 2:42).

The first key to success, "the apostles' teaching," can

Spirit-directed people gear their whole lifestyle and focus toward the purpose of God.

be found today through a relationship with Jesus Christ, the living Word of God, which is strengthened by applying your heart to Bible application and to preaching based on the Word of God.

The second key, "fellowship," simply means hanging out with the sold out—other real followers.

The third key to success is "the breaking of bread." This refers to Holy Communion, which Christians also call the Eucharist and the Lord's Supper.

The fourth key, "the prayers," means talking with God and listening to God. While you can pray as an individual, prayer is also a community experience. It often involves "the prayers" used by the people of God in worship over the centuries.

As Jesus asked, "Is it not written, 'My house shall be called a house of prayer for all the nations'?" (Mark 11:17). The house is not necessarily a physical building. It's the community, the people of God.

Small Groups

All four keys to success can occur in the gathering of the "tribe" for worship. Traditionally worship celebrations happen on Sunday mornings, but many churches today have added Saturday night worship, or perhaps new community times on a weeknight such as Wednesday or Thursday.

These activities also occur in small groups that meet anytime that's workable for the group itself. Many meet in the evening in a home, while others convene in workplaces, restaurants, and fitness clubs.

My challenge to Ginghamsburg Church, when we come together in small classes, teams, or groups, is to make sure we're nurturing God's thoughts. The way we do it is through focusing on the Word of God and prayer. Each group has the same radical teacher—Jesus Christ—and the same overall radical curriculum—the Word of God and prayer.

Too often in churches (including Ginghamsburg), when people get together in groups, they limit themselves to unfocused talking. Soon enough, such groups become places for grumbling and complaining. Folks begin saying critical things like, "I didn't like the new worship songs this week, did you?"

Our curriculum has to be the Word of God and prayer.

When we don't have a radical focus, we start finding fault. Remember, "God's thoughts" do not arise naturally.

If they are to happen, our curriculum has to be the Word of God and prayer. We must look to Jesus as the group's ultimate teacher through the Spirit.

Prayer, even when experienced through small groups, can take time to cultivate. The first followers were willing to do whatever it took to hear from God. When Jesus ascended into heaven, the initial group of believers was a small church of only 120 people. They went back to their meeting place and they "were constantly devoting themselves to prayer" (Acts 1:14).

Jesus ascended into heaven forty days after Easter, and for the next ten days his followers hung out together in a room praying and seeking God's thoughts. Nurturing the thoughts of God does not happen immediately!

> *The first followers were willing to do whatever it took to hear from God. . . . Listening to God takes time.*

If you want to know the mind of God, you can't merely attend church for an hour and then leave. Nor can you join a group and expect instant maturity. This idea of process and time is counter to our microwave, fast food, instant credit, I-want-it-now culture. Listening to God takes time.

Jesus, Our Model

During times of individual prayer, remember the model of Jesus. "In the morning, while it was still very dark, he got up and went out to a deserted place, and there he prayed" (Mark 1:35).

What was he doing before he began the day? He was dream-visioning. He was thinking God's thoughts in order to direct the schedule of his day.

Many people today start their day reading business magazines and listening to business motivational tapes. It is important to look at your business as well through the lens of the Word and the Spirit of God.

Jesus, Our Solution

In one of the stories about the first followers, people are listening to the disciple Peter explain what has happened since God sent the Spirit. Peter says that the Spirit is available to everyone regardless of gender, nationality, age, economics, or education. The Spirit is available to everyone who sincerely calls on the name of the Lord. "Because of what Jesus Christ did, you have the supernatural ability to think God's thoughts" is my summary of what Peter tells them. (See Acts 2.)

"What's the first step for us to take?" the people asked in response. Peter's first word is "Repent." Before their sins are forgiven and they receive the gift of the Holy Spirit, they must repent. (See Acts 2:37-40.)

Repentance means that I have to turn around and change my direction. I have to go on a course that is not comfortable or natural. It is not the path of least resistance. In fact, I will be moving counter to the rest of the culture because I will be surrendered to a God-focus. I will no longer be motivated by self-focus.

Jesus, Our Forgiveness

In spite of our mess-ups, Jesus' followers have the assurance of his love and forgiveness and the promise of his presence. "If we confess our sins, he who is faithful and just will forgive us our sins and cleanse us from all unrighteousness" (1 John 1:9). God is faithful and just to forgive our sins and to cleanse us from any wrong attitude or unhealthy behavior. We have the reminder that we, in the Spirit, have the mind of Christ, the ability to think God's thoughts and to move further toward God's future.

If you need to repent even now, here are some prayer thoughts to assist you or your group: *Lord, many days I run ahead of you. I set out my agenda without knowing your plan or confirming your presence. I don't make sure that I am moving in the direction of your power. Lord, I'm guilty of living my dreams and my passions while merely donating to yours. Instead, I want to totally direct my lifestyle to your purpose. Lord please have mercy on me through the assurance we have in Jesus Christ.*

Network with People Who Share God's Passion

How do we nurture God's dreams, God's visions? We need to find others who share God's passion. You need to network with people who encourage you forward in heaven's mission. That's what mentoring is all about.

You begin to think like the people with whom you spend the majority of your time. If people around you think, "profit, profit, profit," you begin to think, "profit, profit, profit." If your associates are negative, you become negative. If those you hang with are critical, you will soon become critical. We are missing something if we gather in community and then immediately afterward start talking about gossip, investments, or last night's date.

> *You need to network with people who encourage you forward in heaven's mission. That's what mentoring is all about.*

I'd rather hang out with people who throw gasoline on God's fire. What happens if you cannot find enough people that you want to be like? Truth is, there are not enough mentors to go around. As a result, mentoring cannot always be done through one-to-one relationship. You are still responsible for the managing of your own mentoring needs, however. You must still take responsibility for building a network of mentors. I've known people who have been mentored across time and geographic boundaries. I've tried it and it works for me. You may never meet a lot of the people who are part of your mentoring network, but you can read their writings and profit immensely.

Mentor #1: Dietrich Bonhoeffer
Dietrich Bonhoeffer, author of *Cost of Discipleship*, is one of my mentors. Although he died in a concentration camp during World War II, the insights he left behind in his writings and the price he paid for his faith have had a profound effect on me.

Mentor #2: Leonard Sweet
Another one of my mentors is Leonard Sweet, who used to live near me but is now a vice president at Drew University, Madison, New Jersey. I work hard to keep up with Len because he helps me so much with envisioning the future. He also is the person who gave me the opportunity to go to Moscow in 1992 and sit down with Mikhail Gorbachev to discuss the future of Christianity and faith in Russia.

You may never meet a lot of the people that are part of your mentoring network, but you can read their writings.

Len and I may get together only once a year nowadays. Sometimes it's for only twenty minutes at a conference where we're both speaking. But I read everything Len writes (most recently, *Aquachurch*, Group, 1999) and continue to be profoundly mentored by him.

Mentor #3: Lyle Schaller

Another mentor in my life is Lyle Schaller. Lyle is in his seventies and I've been reading his books since seminary, even though I had not met him personally at that time. He has written forty-five books and edited more than forty other books.

When I saw him in Minneapolis in June 1994, I was with several hundred people having hors d'oeuvres at a reception in a hotel. Someone said, "Look over there. That's Lyle Schaller." To my surprise, a few minutes later he walked over to me and said, "Mike Slaughter." I couldn't believe it. He knew my name! He continued, "Your work has inspired so many of us."

He's mentored me through his lifestyle as well as his writing. In 1994, I was invited on a national speaking circuit. My assignment was to tell about some of the things God has been doing and teaching us at Ginghamsburg Church. I started at a low fee, but I quickly learned that other people in this organization were making much more. Some of the "high-visibility" Christian speakers, often from the business arena, received huge amounts a day.

I began to think, *Wow, this is the ladder-climbing business. The better you become, the nicer the cars, houses, and everything else you can provide for your family.* The speaking game was beginning to woo me.

Then I learned a bit more about Lyle Schaller. His books bring in a sizable annual royalty income. Yet he lives in a simple, frame home and he travels around wearing T-shirts rather than designer labels! He doesn't feel pressured to wear $2,000 Armani suits.

I thought, *This man is on a migration in the opposite direction compared to many Christians on the speaking circuit. He is committed to finish strong as a real follower of Jesus Christ.* Lyle's lifestyle of simplicity has significantly influenced me.

Mentor #4: Bob Buford

Another mentor for me is a business leader in Texas named Bob Buford. He got in on the ground floor of the cable industry and built a sizable empire. As a believer, a follower of Jesus, he uses 80 percent of his resources and 80 percent of his time to further the kingdom of God. He even suggests that anyone who has been successful in business ought to live by the 80:20 rule: 80 percent of your time and resources for God and 20 percent for your business, so as to take care of your family. He says that when you die, you want your last check to bounce because you have used all of your resources wisely for God's purpose!

Bob Buford has connected me to incredible leaders. He put me on a team of church leaders who previewed the Hollywood-animated *Moses, Prince of Egypt* film that opened in November 1998. I was glad to have a little input on the film. But I had even more fun developing a new network of mentors as the group of us pastors got to spend time with each other.

You must take responsibility for building your own network of mentors . . . who will encourage you forward toward achieving heaven's mission.

Who Are Your Mentors?

Those are some of my primary mentors. I don't mean to embarrass them by bragging on them. Instead, I want to illustrate how it is possible for people who live far away to play a role in helping shape God's future picture of my life.

Who are the mentors in your life? How are you building a mentoring network? You must take responsibility for building your own network of mentors. This group of persons will encourage you forward toward achieving heaven's mission.

Name Your Mission from God

At the beginning of this chapter I asked you to write out your personal mission. This is different from a life purpose. My life purpose is my overall reason for being here on planet Earth. I believe my life purpose, whether I'm an attorney, a teacher, a dad, or a husband, is to know Christ and to make Christ known. Most statements of life purpose are general and not pegged with a specific activity or roles.

> *My life purpose is my overall reason for being here on planet Earth. Mission, however, is highly specific.*

Mission, however, is highly specific. Your mission is what God wants to do through you in order to accomplish his purpose.

My Mission in the 1970s

When I was nineteen years old my vocation was full-time student and part-time cashier in Cincinnati, but my mission was to turn teenagers in my neighborhood into real followers of Jesus. I had started a teen movement and opened a teen club. I had gone around town raising money to buy a pool table and air hockey tables, and I began to work with youth.

We held Bible studies for the teens. This was a time when my community experienced racial conflict, so we brought white kids and black kids together in the name and power of Jesus.

One of our young people was named Jerry. His dad earned minimum wage working in a foundry. Jerry would never have been able to go to college, so I found ways to raise money for him to attend. When I was twenty-one, Carolyn and I married. We didn't have much money, but our mission was still to turn kids in our neighborhood into real followers of Jesus. After our first year of marriage, we moved to Asbury Seminary in Kentucky, but we drove back into Ohio every weekend in order to work with the same kids.

In time Jerry became a student at Asbury College in Kentucky (and eventually a missionary to Korea). Even though we were also students and had no extra money, we would take Jerry down to Dawahare's in Lexington and buy him clothes and shoes so he could go to school. Our life's focus went into God's focus.

Your Mission in the Millennium

When you identify your mission, it will probably be as specific as mine. Your mission will come out of your passion. It is something that you are drawn to. It will probably be something connected to your life and ministry experiences to date. It will also be something you feel is a gift from God. Ultimately, when you're listening to the Spirit of God, you can't keep from doing whatever it is that God is calling you to do.

Your mission will come out of your passion. It is something that you are drawn to.

Notice the sidebar featuring Mark Stephenson. As a technical director of research and development, Mark's spiritual passion is close to his vocation. Yet it is distinct in how he uniquely contributes to the kingdom of God.

Mark began this ministry as an unpaid servant. He didn't sit around wondering what he was supposed to

Mark Stephenson: A Real Follower Who Has Impact on the World

When my wife and I attended membership classes in 1994, we were asked to find our gifts. I kept feeling that my gifts didn't fit the things that were happening at the church.

One Sunday I heard Mike Slaughter say, "God has spoken to me to reach 10,000 people for Jesus Christ." I'm an electrical engineer who works for a high-tech research and technology company. It dawned on me that we could use the Internet to have an impact far beyond what we could ever achieve with our current buildings.

I developed a few sample Web pages, showed them to staff, and it took off from there. The CyberMinistry is redefining the ministry of the local church. Originally we thought it would serve primarily the people of our church, but it turns out that at least 70 percent of our Internet guests aren't even from Ohio.

We launched in 1997, and by May 1999 we hit 20,000 web visitors a month, representing forty countries. By early 1999 more than 500 people experienced our worship services on the Internet each week. We created over 1,000 Web pages as a totally lay ministry. Then in 1999 I came on Ginghamsburg staff one day a week as the director of CyberMinistry.

Until the CyberMinistry emerged, no ministries in the church fit me. I wanted to be involved in ministry, and I did participate, but it never worked well. The CyberMinistry, on the other hand, is very natural. God designed and prepared me for this ministry.

It is exciting to use technology for Jesus. The reward of doing it for Jesus is what rewards me.

do for God. It came out of his passion and out of his giftedness.

Your Mission and Your Employment

Will living out your mission cause you to leave your job and seek employment at a church or ministry? Perhaps not. Look at the influence of teachers like Tony Compolo, a professor of sociology at Eastern College who has gifts of evangelism and writing. In the realm of politics, Tony Hall, elected to the U.S. Congress from our area, is a real follower of Jesus Christ. He is doing a great job combating world hunger. Look at what Elizabeth Dole has done through the Red Cross. Deion Sanders, a professional athlete, had a life-changing experience with Jesus Christ in recent years. It is amazing how that man's life has been transformed. Check out all the endeavors he puts his heart into besides baseball and football.

Decide who your mentors will be depending on what business you're in. Choose people in your mentoring network who can help you name your mission. One of the most significant things that you'll ever do with your life is to become an active part of a local church, one that exudes excitement about what God is doing in its people and community.

Decide who your mentors will be depending on what business you're in.

God created you with a mission. If you accept that mission, your life will be a miracle to many people. Your mission, should you choose to accept it, is to use your gifts to carry out God's dream. In the power of the Holy Spirit, you can make a difference in your world.

Identify your mission and serve God by serving people.

That journey will be the most significant experience of your entire life.

Discussion Questions

1. *What small group (class, team) has been most helpful in your journey to become a real follower of Jesus? How have the people or accountabilities of that group spurred you forward?*

2. *Who has been your most significant mentor in recent years? How did you happen to select that person? How has he or she influenced you most strongly?*

3. *Who else would you like to mentor you? What obstacle or fear keeps you from building a stronger relationship with that person?*

4. *If you're meeting in a group, ask how you can pray for one another. Pray together.*

Joining the Movement

 What could your entire church do to challenge and change the culture around you?

Example: Does the small group you're most active in ever have a time of setting goals or reviewing its covenant? Why not show the section of this chapter on small groups (pages 71-72) to your small-group leader, asking if time in a future meeting could be given to a discussion of this question: "How could we improve our group so that each of us is even more helped to become real followers of Christ?"

Example: What would happen if your church became more intentional about building mentoring networks? Check with your pastor or, as appropriate, one of the key teachers or preachers in your faith community. Ask if any upcoming focus would tie into the idea of mentoring. If so, why not suggest a "month of mentoring" emphasis where people are encouraged to approach one another for an experimental month of one-on-one mentoring? Any relationships that click could, of course, continue beyond that month.

Chapter Five

Experiencing the Power of Amazing Grace

*Today's culture of "ungrace" is a perfectionist one
where value is tied to appearance and performance.
As a follower of Christ, we are not accepted by God
because we are right or good. We are accepted by
God because we are forgiven. To what extent are
you living in forgiveness?*

What made the movie *Forrest Gump* become one of the biggest hits of our time? Forrest is a kid with a low IQ. Yet he ends up becoming the winner in numerous impossible-type situations. He accomplishes more with his life than hundreds of "normal" people.

He wins in all of his relationships, saves his buddy in Vietnam, coins popular slogans, launches a lucrative business, helps people in need, and is faithful to his friend Jenny in spite of her unfaithfulness. He seems unaware that he is the butt of everyone's jokes.

A clue to his success appears in one of the earliest scenes in the movie. When young Forrest catches his leg braces in a sewer grate, a couple of bystanders stare at his handicapped condition. As Forrest and his mother walk away, she counsels her teachable son: "Don't ever let anyone tell you they're better than you, boy. If God had intended everyone to be the same, he'd have made everyone with braces on their legs."

You Have Great Value to God

Forrest went through life with an attitude that "Mama was always right." His "mama" had a profound impact on his sense of esteem, worth, and value.

You and I are created "in the image of God" (Gen 1:27). God, in creating the human race, "breathed into his nostrils the breath of life; and the man became a living being" (Gen. 2:7). That breath is the esteem and worth of what it means to be a child of God.

That sense of value comes from God. "Are not two sparrows sold for a penny? Yet not one of them will fall to the ground apart from your Father. . . . You are of more value than many sparrows" (Matt. 10:29-31).

While our value, esteem, and worth come from God, they are nurtured by humans, usually in a home environment, just as in the case of Forrest Gump.

The power to shape another person's self-perception is something God wants us to use for good. Jesus communicates this idea with words that I believe apply to every generation of real followers. Jesus came back from the dead and gave his first followers some "Don't fear" words of assurance. Then Jesus says, "If you forgive the sins of any, they are forgiven them; if you retain the sins of any, they are retained" (John 20:23).

God Gives You Power

What power! Jesus gives his followers the power to hurt or to heal, to bless or to curse. If they hang on to unforgiveness, then the cycle of unforgiveness will be retained. They can also forgive, and in doing so model what it means to receive God's grace.

Real followers become people of amazing grace. Jesus restores what God gave to us as human beings at the creation but was lost in our brokenness.

Jesus rebuilds in his followers the sense of esteem for what it means to be God's children. Then he shows his concern about relationships by sending us out with power to hurt or to heal, to bless or to curse through our relationships.

Jesus gives his followers the power to hurt or to heal, to bless or to curse.

This is an awesome responsibility! These powers of blessing are just the opposite of what you might call today's culture of "ungrace."

Notice the Impact of Your Culture

We live in a perfectionist culture where value is tied to appearance and performance. Diseases such as anorexia have been born out of today's culture because we set up unrealistic ideas of body shape and size. We think we need to be incredibly thin in order to be accepted.

You Are Grouped and Graded

Very early in our lives, we are grouped and graded. These assessments have a major influence on how we feel about ourselves.

Who can forget going to first grade and being sorted between different reading groups? My teachers tried to disguise it, but it didn't work. We had the Aardvark Group, the Bumble Bee Group, the Caterpillar Group. It didn't take a rocket scientist to figure out that the Caterpillars were slower than the Aardvarks.

I was always in the "C" group. I could tell that my group ranking was of great concern to my mother. She wanted me to get into a better group so I would have a better chance at college.

As a result of experiences like these, we grow up with

the idea that our esteem and value are tied to our performance. We begin to think that we need to contribute something in order to be accepted.

We then carry into adulthood the idea that our self-image is tied to what we do and how we do it. For example, Carolyn always phones me when I am traveling. Her standard question is, "How did it go today?" She asks that because she knows how important it is to me that my speaking engagements go well. She asks the same after I've spoken at church. I want God to work through me and Carolyn knows that. The underlying truth is that my feelings about myself are related to how I perform.

> *We grow up with the idea that our esteem and value are tied to our performance.*

You Pass These Attitudes to Your Children

We then continue the cycle by passing these values to our children. When Jonathan has a baseball game, we know that 2 hits for 4 at bats is a good day but 0 for 4 is a bad day. If he has a 3-for-4 day, we know he'll be feeling great. His sense of esteem is shaped by his performance and appearance.

The problem is that life contains many 0-for-4 days for most people. We don't feel good again until we have a few more "hits." Our esteem and value is so tied to how we behave that it can determine how we feel about ourselves.

Behind this feeling that we have to perform is the message, "I must *do* something to be accepted." This culture-of-ungrace chain continues from parent to child from one generation to another.

Learn to Accept God's Grace

We live in a culture of ungrace, but the follower of Jesus
serves a God of grace. God shows us an unconditional
love. "But God proves his love for us in that while we still
were sinners Christ died for us" (Rom. 5:8). This is why
we can be people of grace in a culture of ungrace.

Don't Let Culture Define God

Yet that is not how most people think about God.
Instead, we often take our image of God from our culture.
Many people's dominant picture of God is someone who
gives them what they earn. "I am going to reap what I
sow," we believe.

That image, if not tempered by a sense of God's unde-
served favor, creates fear and intimidation. In our deepest beings, we have a need to know that God accepts us,
owns us, holds us, and affirms us even when he is not too
impressed with the way we act at any given time.

*Grace means
I won't reap
what I sow.
Does God
accept me
because
I am good
and right?
No! It's because
I am forgiven.*

Grace means I don't get
what I deserve. Grace
means I won't reap what I
sow. "For by grace you
have been saved through
faith, and this is not your
own doing; it is the gift of
God" (Eph. 2:8).

Does God accept me
because I am already good
and right? No! It's because
I am forgiven.

Jesus Christ died on the cross so that I can be accepted
by God. Through Jesus, my relationship with heaven is
just as if I had never done anything to wrong God. Jesus
Christ bridges the gap between God and humanity.

There is nothing I can do to earn God's favor. The mathematics of God's grace leads to the statement, "You are forgiven."

Don't Live by the Mathematics of Karma

Instead of living in the truth of God's grace and forgiveness, people like me tend to live by the mathematics of karma. This Hindu concept is plain and simple: you get what you earn, you reap what you sow. Karma provides the formula that you and I need 6.8 million rebirths to make up for this lifetime's mistakes.

God does not love or forgive me because I am right or good. Grace says that nothing I do can make God love me more or less.

Imagine yourself as a father who invests your life in your children. You've made great personal sacrifices so they can have music lessons, join sports teams, and ultimately go to college. Now, in the middle of his junior year, one of your sons drops out of college. Using moneys he's been given for future tuition, he moves off campus, gets in with the wrong crowd, and becomes a party animal. He takes your car and ruins your reputation. His physical appearance suggests that he might have contracted a sexually transmitted disease.

Somewhere along the line, this kid comes to the place where he realizes he is not making it. He recognizes that he has a hole in his soul. He begins a quest for God.

That is where many people in our culture are today. Our culture is hungry for spiritual truth.

Don't Decide That God Will Reject You

In a similar story that Jesus told, the son set out on a quest back to his father. If the story were set today, you as the father might ask, "What happened to my car?" or "Are you going back to college yet?" or "Which girl are you living with now?" or "Are you still struggling with your addictions?" or "Is that pot I smell?" or even "Why have you wasted your life?" Maybe you would have no interest in your son anymore.

None of that anger or criticism appears in Jesus' story. Instead, "while he was still far off, his father saw him and was filled with compassion; he ran and put his arms around him and kissed him" (Luke 15:20).

I am amazed by the father's response. Often, I cannot understand why God refrains from giving me what I deserve. I can't imagine that I won't reap what I sow.

What an incredible God! This is the message of grace that Jesus wants his followers to convey.

"As the Father has sent me, so I send you," he tells us. He then gives us the power we need: "Receive the Holy Spirit." What is his purpose? We can now model forgiveness in a culture of ungrace. "If you forgive the sins of any, they are forgiven them; if you retain the sins of any, they are retained."

Model Grace to Others

You and I are to comprise the community of the people of grace. C. S. Lewis, Oxford professor and author of The Chronicles of Narnia, started his life as an agnostic and ended up a very strong disciple of Jesus Christ. I love how he described the life of grace. He said, "To be a Christian means to forgive the inexcusable because God has forgiven the inexcusable in you."

> **C. S. Lewis said:**
> *"To be a Christian means to forgive the inexcusable because God has forgiven the inexcusable in you."*

In other words, you didn't get what you deserved. You didn't reap what you sowed. You have received freely, so you should give freely. Because you are forgiven, you understand how to show forgiveness to other people.

Religious People Have Trouble with Grace

Tony Campolo, a sociologist who teaches at Eastern College in Pennsylvania, enjoys speaking at secular colleges. He often asks students, "What is Jesus about?" He is amazed by how few understand the ways that Jesus is unique. One of Jesus' distinctive teach-

We are to call no one unclean.

ings is his command to "love and forgive your enemies." Jesus alone teaches us that no one is beyond hope. We are to call no one unclean. That is one way Jesus' teachings are unique from any other religious leader in the world.

Guess who has the most trouble accepting this call to unconditional love? Religious people. People who supposedly have freely received are constantly battling with what it means to be forgiven and to forgive others.

This dilemma is not new. The same thing happened in Jesus' day. He became so irate at certain religious leaders one time that he said to some priests: ". . . the tax collectors and the prostitutes are going into the kingdom of God ahead of you" (Matt. 21:31).

Why would Jesus say that? People who had fallen hard and low understood the idea of receiving freely. They knew that they had not gotten what they deserved. They were deeply appreciative of God's promise that they were not going to reap what they had sowed.

Religious People Can Be "Bigger Pains"

When I'm being interviewed for newspaper articles, I like to ask the reporter if he or she is part of a faith community that follows Jesus. I remember one who said no; she had grown up in the church, but now she is a

Cynthia Swann:
A Real Follower Who Reaches
Out to People in Need

I grew up in a family that talked about God, but didn't have a relationship with Jesus Christ. In college I remember getting off a phone conversation with my boyfriend (now husband) about Jesus being the Son of God. "I don't understand, please reveal this to me," I bawled that night in prayer, begging to God for forgiveness. I realized that Jesus had been there all along, walking me through every step in my life to bring me to this point. It was the biggest turning point in my life.

Later I took a job in Dayton. A friend invited me to a Bible study at work and later invited me to church. The welcoming atmosphere of my first visit was enough to keep me going.

I now serve the church as a lay pastor. People come to us who need assistance with rent or other vital needs. I've been trained to pray with them and then to help line up resources that can pay their light bill or get them access to a food pantry.

Then I take it a step farther. I do a follow-up to make sure they're okay. On several occasions, I've driven out to someone's home. I helped one person study for the high school equivalency exam.

Interviewing people about their needs is uncomfortable. I try to build a relationship, showing the beauty of Christ. They're at their lowest, and I don't want them to feel turned away or judged. I see God at work each time I step out of my comfort zone to break down those barriers.

Buddhist. One of the reasons she gave for leaving her church was that people in the congregation lacked compassion.

I agree with the reporter of another paper, the *San Francisco Chronicle*, who said the problem with born-again people is that they are a bigger pain the "second time around."

It doesn't have to be that way. Real followers have the power available to model forgiveness and grace.

In fact, Jesus calls his followers to create the kind of "safe space" zones where grace and forgiveness are the rule. Our homes, and our relationships are to demonstrate God's grace and forgiveness to the world—not fear, not intimidation, and not judgment.

Invite People into Your Safe-Space Zone

Church people symbolize safe-space zones when they present their children for baptism or dedication. The message of the ceremony says to these kids, "You live in a culture of ungrace, but you represent the kingdom of grace. You now have a mark from God that reminds you of forgiveness and grace. God has created you with a tremendous future with a tremendous plan and a hope. God does not want you to fail."

In every way, we want to communicate to our friends, relatives, and children, "God has an incredible plan for your life."

Then, as we bring up our children in God's ways, we are really acting as God's nannies. We are responsible for shaping their self-esteem in the midst of a world of ungrace. We are sensitive to anything that would criticize or tear down. In every way, we want to communicate to our friends, relatives, and children, "God has an incredible plan for your life."

Problem is, we mess up. You do, and I do too.

One Sunday morning, I asked Jonathan, who was sixteen at the time, to cut our grass at home after church before the afternoon rains came. Keeping up the yard is one of the regular chores we pay him to do. It had poured rain all week, and the lawn looked like a hay field. Monday is the only day I take off, and I didn't want to spend it cutting grass.

At church, one of his friends invited him out to a birthday dinner. He came home mid-afternoon to work on the yard, but by that time it was already pouring. That meant I had to spend the next day, my day off, mowing—doing Jonathan's job.

When Jonathan came home from school on Monday, I cut into him. I didn't pause to ask about his day. I blasted him. My words blamed and shamed, and I got mean.

Later Carolyn said to me, "You went beyond teaching that young man responsibility." She was right. Jesus gave people the power to hurt or heal, to curse or bless. I made the wrong choice. I failed to behave as God's nanny.

We all blow it. That doesn't mean we should quit. Jesus commissions us—"As the Father has sent me, so I send you." He equips us—blowing on us with the Holy Spirit, the presence of God. He sends us with a message to a world that is wrapped tight with shame and pain. He tells us that if we forgive the sins of any, they will be forgiven. If we hang on to the sins of any, they will be retained.

Becoming a Safe-Space Zone

How can we be a safe-space zone of forgiveness and grace for someone? For one, we need time.

I remember watching a television news magazine interview with outgoing congressman Joseph Kennedy. "Aren't you going to miss voting with Congress?" the interviewer asked.

He replied, "When I get to the end of my life, I don't think

I'm ever going to be sorry that I missed one more vote or one more meeting. The event I will probably be sorry I missed is being present for my son's football games."

Second, to become a safe-space zone, we need focus. Notice how many times Jesus healed people. The Scriptures note: "Jesus looked at them and then said . . ." His eye contact suggests that he gave them his full attention and presence. By contrast, how many times do we treat people as an interruption to something more important?

Third, just as the father ran to his son and hugged him, we create safe-space zones through meaningful touch. I remember a particularly tense week that Carolyn and I experienced. There was lots of activity happening through the church. We were sitting in a park, and she became a bit teary. She said, "I don't know what's wrong with me, but I think it's just that I'm missing my hugs." (So I hugged her.)

How many times do we get going in hectic schedules and we don't pay attention to meaningful touch? Meaningful touch can clearly be distinguished from sexual harassment. Even in church contexts, the wrong kind of squeeze is never appropriate.

A fourth way to create safe space is to speak of a God-centered future. You may be in pain over a broken relationship with a spouse, child, friend, or relative. You may be grieving, but you too can speak of the future with hope. Affirm to your children and to the people closest to you your faith dreams of what God has created them to become. For example, you could say, "God's hand is all over you. You're going to do great things for God." People become what we speak.

Finally, act out of commitment to build a safe-space zone. Spend time with neighbors, colleagues at work, and family members. Serve them with acts of kindness. Show interest in their world. Include people in groups and events that are part of your community of faith.

If you're a parent, you may tell your children that they have all the talent in the world. What you need to do is pay the $68 a month for piano lessons. Act out of a commitment to fulfill that special future. My son likes to play baseball. He has a goal to play at the college level. I have pitched thousands of balls during the season. I wasn't a good ballplayer, but I want him to know how much I care about what's important in his life.

We live in a culture of ungrace, but we are a community of grace. We are the people of grace.

Breaking the Cycle

Today you can break the cycle of withheld forgiveness and failure to show grace. Through Jesus, you have the power to break the chains that tie up those you love and care about. You have the privilege of declaring a special future for someone else, and trusting God to see it come to pass.

You don't have to hang on to resentment, bitterness, and pain, nor does it need to continue being passed from parent to child for many generations. You don't have to act like the surrounding world of ungrace.

Are you willing to declare today as the time that the cycle has broken? If so, would you be willing to talk to God in prayer? Before you pray, try to identify a significant relationship that you will give to God. Choose one in which you have failed. Maybe you shamed and blamed. You have tied value to appearance and performance with this individual. You have wrongfully modeled the lie that we are accepted by God because we are right or good rather than because we are forgiven.

Lord Jesus, I confess to you that I have blown it. Through my anger and my pain and my other unresolved stuff, I have contributed to blaming and sham-

*ing one of your children, who is created in your image.
I offer this person who I named before you. I ask you
for the strength to be a safe-space zone for this person.
I ask that even in my anger, pain, or confusion, I will
speak only words of grace and of acceptance and forgiveness.*

*I entrust this person to your created purpose. I
believe you want to use me in this person's life for
good, for kingdom success, and to honor you. I pray
that your will, your purpose, and your pardon be com-
pleted in this life in the name of Jesus. Amen.*

Discussion Questions

1. *When was your first awareness in life that most people accept you on the basis of how you look or perform, more than on the basis of who you are?*

2. *What does it mean to you to be created "in the
   image of God"? Can you give an example from your
   life of the following sentences? "Real followers
   become people of amazing grace. Jesus restores
   what God gave to us as human beings at the creation but was lost in our brokenness."*

3. *At the end of the chapter, you were asked to pray for
   someone toward whom you have not modeled grace,
   forgiveness, or acceptance. Who did you select and why?*

4. *If you're meeting in a group, ask how you can pray
   for one another. Pray together.*

Joining the Movement

 What could your entire church do to challenge
and change the culture around you?

Example: How could you help your faith community convey the safe-space zone idea of this chapter? If you have an outdoor church message board, could you obtain permission to feature words like "a people of forgiveness and acceptance"? If you have a church newsletter or mailings, what wording could be used to show that your church is a safe-space zone where grace and forgiveness are the rule?

Example: Could you use some outside help in showing grace, forgiveness, and acceptance to someone who continually bothers you? Who is it that represents an ongoing struggle for you, the kind that causes emotions to swell, hair to stand on end, or fitful sleeping? Get some help, such as from a counselor that your pastor can refer you to. Then, when God grants you victory, tell it to your small group or church as a whole. Tell others how God has changed your attitude and enabled you to break a damaging cycle.

Chapter Six

"God-Sizing" Your Visions and Dreams

When you order lunch, certain restaurants ask if you want your order supersized. Likewise, when you dream about your life purpose, make sure you "God-size" it. Faith communities are here not to help you articulate a vision for personal success and a plan for getting rich, but to help you grasp a picture of God's future for your life. The issue isn't about bringing Jesus into our plans and dreams. It's about surrendering our plan for God's intent.

D o you ever do homework for personal growth? Lots of adults do. They study something unrelated to their line of work, go to a museum, take a class, or watch a series of educational broadcasts or videos.

Maybe you're thinking, *Mike, I hate to tell you this, but I'm done with school. I'm a grown-up.* That last word can be a problem. The tense of the term *grown-up* implies that we have stopped developing. It communicates the idea that we've arrived. When you or I stop learning, we stop growing and changing. As UCLA's John Wooden says, "It's what you learn after you know it all that counts."

> **The tense of the term grown-up implies that we have stopped developing. ... When you or I stop learning, we stop growing and changing.**

Children dream. They have an incredible ability to imagine the future. They're great at make-believe. They enjoy role-playing. That's the way God wired us when we were born.

The Bible says, "Where there is no vision, the people perish" (Prov. 29:18 KJV). Without dreams, we become stagnant. Our life journey becomes severely limited.

Recently, I saw a newspaper headline that said 2,000 students had rioted at Ohio University and the police had to fire rubber bullets to stop them. Eight other major universities had similar riots.

What was the issue? In the riots of the 1960s students were protesting the Vietnam War and the draft. I read the newspaper article to find out what everyone was so concerned about on these nine campuses. Do you know what sparked the rioting? The right to have beer bashes!

Talk about lack of vision. This small-mindedness isn't limited to students. I can't believe the number of people at midlife who have no passion. They are employed, but they are burned out or unfocused because nothing big has captured their dreams.

Dream God's Dream

The Spirit's invasion enables Jesus' followers to think God's thoughts.

Shortly after Jesus went back up to heaven, God sent the Spirit to live inside Jesus' followers. This happened during a religious festival known as Pentecost.

The Spirit's invasion enables Jesus' followers to think God's thoughts. Through the presence of the Holy Spirit "we have the mind of Christ" (1 Cor. 2:16).

Jesus' followers can also read God's heart. "I will put

my laws in their minds, and write them on their hearts" (Heb. 8:10).

If the Spirit controls you, truths about God are no longer written only on tablets of stone or ancient parchments. Now you can think God's thoughts—present tense—for the purpose of living God's future for your life.

Human vision by itself is flawed because of self-focus. Human vision always comes down to what *I* want to do, what *I* want to have, and where *I* want to be. Self is at the center. Our benchmarks and goals are likewise based on self-focus.

Human vision is fueled by Madison Avenue. From birth, we are bombarded with advertisements. The typical person receives some 17,000 messages each day, if you count commercials, billboards, Internet banners, magazine ads, and the like. In the United States of America, the average child sees 15,000 to 30,000 hours of television between childhood and age seventeen.

Most ads sell an image. For example, what's the craze behind sport-utility vehicles (SUVs)? Advertisements teach us that if we buy one, we can experience the spirit of adventure. The pitch comes from unusual, off-road places like mountaintops, even though most of us never really plan to go off-road with our SUVs! Apparently, the thought of that experience is enough to persuade us to buy an SUV.

North Americans keep wanting whatever Madison Avenue dishes out, so most of us live beyond our means. I'm shocked by the number of people I talk to who have household incomes of more than six figures but who can't pay their bills.

Ironically, our generation demands all these conveniences, but the typical work week is growing, not shrinking. We are working longer and harder than our parents to support a lifestyle, but we are not really living.

Bigger Than Madison Avenue

God created you and me for the purpose of intimate companionship. In our brokenness—our desire to be self-sufficient and independent, to be like God—that closeness was shattered.

God created you and me for the purpose of intimate companionship. In our brokenness—our desire to be self-sufficient —that closeness was shattered.

Faith communities are not here week after week to help you articulate a vision for personal success and a plan for getting rich. If I was into that I'd be doing infomercials. Rather, the goal is to help you connect to God's dream, to grasp a picture of God's future, to see how your life fits into God's plan and how your life can count for God's purpose. The idea is not to bring Jesus into our plans and dreams. It's about surrendering our plan for his. It starts with dreaming God's dreams.

God's dreams tend to be bigger than the power of our imagination. That's why we need supernatural intervention. Otherwise we're limited by our own finite thinking. We can't dream bigger than our imaginations will allow.

The following problem shows how narrow and limited human thinking tends to be. (If you have done this exercise before and you've forgotten the answer, you confirm my point because you've gone back to your limited thinking.)

The challenge is to connect the nine dots on the top of page 103 with four straight lines. You must not lift your pencil or pen, and your lines must be straight.

I tried and failed. Then I cheated and used five lines.

● ● ●

● ● ●

● ● ●

Turn to page 116 to find the solution. If you're like me, the reason you failed is because your mind confined itself to an invisible box around the nine dots. We were locked in a box of invisible boundaries.

To solve the problem, I had to break past the invisible barrier that the mind set up. We need whole-brain thinking. For the Christian this consists of left brain (the logical, detailed side), right brain (the creative side), and Spirit (the mind of Christ). We have infinite possibilities through the mind of Christ.

In many cases, if you want to dream God's dream, you must be willing to think outside your limited, human box.

Articulate God's Dream

Not only do you need to dream God's dream, but you need to articulate it. Chapter 4 of this book helped you begin to write out God's mission for your life.

Hopefully, you have been learning how to simplify your life so as to hear God more clearly. We can busy ourselves doing good things that we miss God's things. Good is often the enemy of best.

When to Say "No" or "Yes"

No is an important word to learn. Jesus understood it, though his first followers sometimes did not. Jesus would go away to pray, to dream a vision by listening to the thoughts of God. The disciples, led by Simon Peter, knew that many people were looking for Jesus—people with all kinds of good work for him to become involved in. "And Simon and his companions hunted for him. When they found him, they said to him, 'Everyone is searching for you.' He answered, 'Let us go on to the neighboring towns, so that I may proclaim the message there also; for that is what I came out to do.'

When you articulate your life purpose, make sure to "God-size" it.

And he went throughout Galilee, proclaiming the message in their synagogues and casting out demons" (Mark 1:36-39).

Jesus knew his life purpose. It enabled him to narrow his focus and say no to the good so that he could do the best. It is important that you articulate your life purpose.

When you articulate your life purpose, make sure to "God-size" it. When you go into certain fast-food restaurants, they ask if you want your order supersized. I tell people, "If you become part of this community of faith, then expect to experience a God-sizing of your vision and dreams." The translation for those reading this book? Hang out with people who think big; beware of small-minded, no-risk, cautious atmospheres.

When you dream God's dream, you'll see how it differs from little, dinky infomercial strategies for personal success and wealth.

When you dream and articulate God's dream, it will be contagious! You will infect other people around you. That's good, because often the dream is too big for you alone or for you to accomplish in your lifetime.

Look at Mother Teresa. I studied some of her earliest experiences. They seem to be average at best. Colleagues in her convent remarked that she was nothing special as a student, teacher, or person. (How would you like that to be written about you?)

But Mother Teresa connected to the Spirit, dreamed God's dream, and changed her focus. She didn't go with the self-comfort movement. She went in the opposite direction from the culture of self-focus. She received a special calling from God to reach out to the poorest of the poor.

When Mother Teresa died, barefoot paupers, movie stars, and government officials waited outside in monsoon rains for hours for a chance to file by her body. She was given a state funeral by the Indian government, an honor usually reserved for heads of state. Three months before her death, she received the Nobel Peace Prize.

Why was this Nobel Peace Prize recipient held in such high esteem and honor by people of all faiths and stations in life? Because Mother Teresa dreamed God's dream and acted on God's vision.

Act on God's Dream

First, dream the vision of God. Second, articulate the vision of God. Third, act on the vision of God.

God shares his vision and dream with people who passionately want to do God's purposes. For example, Isaiah the prophet describes an experience in the temple of God, which would be equivalent to Christians in worship today. "Then I heard the voice of the LORD saying, 'Whom shall I send, and who will go for us?' And I said, 'Here am I; send me!' " (Isa. 6:8).

God shares his vision and dream with people who passionately want to do God's purposes.

Notice his immediate response of a willingness to act. That's how we need to answer: "Whatever it takes, whatever it costs, I don't care. I just want to know your dream. I want to live your vision. Life is too short. I want to be used for your purpose."

Do you long to be used by God? Then when you hear God's voice, your heart will scream, with the prophet Isaiah, "Here I am, use me!"

Bigger Than I

During my senior year in high school I went to a party one Saturday night down in someone's basement. We were doing things that we shouldn't have been doing. Drunkenness and "dark" things were going on.

I sat looking at my friends and my girlfriend. This vision or idea came to me that we were all lost. It was as if we were in a dark room bouncing off each other, bouncing off the walls, trying to find the doorway out. But no one could find the exit. Later, I would decide that it was God communicating with me.

On Monday afternoon at North College Hill High School, I walked with my girlfriend around the southeast corner of the high school building. I remember the exact location. As I went around the corner and passed by a certain bush, I had a God moment. I believe God spoke to me.

This was amazing because at that point I had never had an experience with Jesus Christ. Yet I believe God said to me, "I'm going to use you to lead people out of darkness." I later learned that the Bible is full of examples of how God spoke through people even when they had not put their trust in him.

I had been on my way to art class. I was taking every possible course that could raise my average and get me the credits I needed to graduate. It seemed like an otherwise perfectly normal day.

My girlfriend and I had never before had a spiritual conversation. She must have thought I had gone crazy, because I looked at her and said, "I'm supposed to be a minister."

Bigger Than You

A God moment is when you sense God's call in a personal way and from that time on everything changes—your identity, who you are, what you do. The experience marks a radical paradigm shift.

All of us have a mission from God, a mission in life. God has been "cooking" this in you since you were born. It can be traced back to some early passion that you have had in your life. Moses began with a passion. As he was growing up in Egypt, he was troubled about the oppression of his people, the Jews. This concern bubbled inside him, showing him that he had a bigger mission than merely serving Pharaoh as prince of Egypt.

A God moment is when you sense God's call in a personal way and from that time on everything changes— your identity, who you are, what you do.

He didn't understand that his life's mission was bigger than he could accomplish alone. So he took matters into his own hands and miserably failed. He killed an Egyptian, for which he was eventually disowned and exiled into the desert. (See his story in Exodus 1–3.)

Moses, like many of us today, found himself years later living an existence far removed from his original passion. Also like Moses, you and I tend to limit our mission to what we believe we can accomplish with the resources and strengths we have as human beings.

Moses was eighty years old when God spoke to him from a burning bush. Like us, when he heard God speak Moses' first response was resistance. Moses said to God, "Who am I that I should go to Pharaoh, and bring the Israelites out of Egypt?" (Exod. 3:11).

As Moses did, we also ask, "Why me, God?" We limit ourselves by our past failures and the feelings of inadequacies that we have about ourselves. Unfulfilled childhood needs and esteem issues are all factors that affect our ideas of what our life mission will be.

You and I tend to limit our mission to what we believe we can accomplish with the resources and strengths we have as human beings.

Moses did indeed face some major impediments. He was born a slave, and he was a stutterer. He overcame these impediments to become the leader God used to thwart the mightiest country of the day.

Our picture of the future is always limited. God's picture for Moses was bigger than Moses could envision. Moses could imagine being prince of Egypt, but he couldn't conceive of what God had in mind.

Beyond You and Me

God has a life mission for you and me and it is bigger than we can imagine. One drawback is that we tend to limit ourselves to common sense.

Jesus had a friend named Lazarus who was very sick and dying. So his two sisters, Martha and Mary, sent for Jesus. By the time Jesus got there, Lazarus was dead. His funeral had been conducted and his body had been wrapped up and put to rest in a cave, sealed with a huge stone. Jesus' response was to say, "Take away the stone" (John 11:39).

Martha limited herself to common sense. She told Jesus, "Lord, already there is a stench because he has been dead four days" (John 11:39).

Martha's mental picture was limited, but God's was bigger. They moved the stone. Jesus prayed and said, "Lazarus, come out!" (John 11:43). The dead man arose.

Martha had voiced at least three concerns: (1) "We can't open the tomb"; (2) "It will stink"; and (3) "You're too late; he's been dead for days."

"Jesus said to her, 'Did I not tell you that if you believed, you would see the glory of God?' " (John 11:40). What he's referring to is living as children of a larger God. Your life mission is not limited to what you can imagine about yourself. What can you do with your life? Don't picture only what you can imagine. The issue is what God imagines about you! We are children of a larger God.

What can you do with your life? Don't picture only what you can imagine. The issue is what God imagines about you!

"I Don't Have the Right Degree"

"I can't." "I'm too old." "I don't have the right degree." "It won't work." All these phrases stem from intelligence without God. Two of the key staff roles at Ginghamsburg Church are presently filled by women who could have used every common-sense excuse imaginable. Had they followed sheer logic, they would have missed God's dream for what they could do.

Tammy Kelley was a dental hygienist for seventeen years, was divorced, and didn't put her trust in Jesus until about age twenty-five. Kim Miller had lots of informal training in drama and in the way churches should work, but she was a licensed practical nurse by profession. As their profiles indicate (see sidebars on pages 110 and 111), these two are critical to the leadership of Ginghamsburg Church, and yet there's not an advanced degree between them.

Tammy Kelley: A Real Follower Who Empowers Others

My first role at the church was to hand out worship bulletins. My husband and I, along with our three children, began attending Ginghamsburg in 1989. As already-committed Christians, we were first attracted to Ginghamsburg because Jesus is so real here and because the "priesthood of all believers" is such a driving force.

I am a homegrown staff person. In 1995, after seventeen years as a dental hygienist, I had the opportunity to join the staff team at Ginghamsburg, first as a parttimer unpaid, and eventually as paid full-time. My responsibilities as Executive Director include staff and organizational development, equipping people for ministry, and leadership development.

I have a passion for ministering to people who have been previously unchurched and for making church a relevant community. My overall ministry goal is to help people find significant places of connection, community, and service through teams and groups.

I am not an ordained clergywoman, but because of my giftedness and the fact that my church embraces the priesthood of all believers, I have had the opportunity to have a key leadership role here. I use the same leadership development tools when working with our paid staff as I do when working with the church's unpaid servants. All are empowered and equipped to serve according to their gifts and passion.

With Jesus life has purpose. There is nothing else I would rather be doing.

**Kim Miller: A Real Follower
Who Spurs Creativity**

I became a follower of Christ in high school. I had found a book on my mom's shelf and I began reading *The Robe.* Night after night, I looked forward to experiencing more. The unfolding story made me very aware that Jesus is real. I began a journey strangely warmed by the presence of God.

My role on staff is called Creative Worship Director. I dream with the teaching pastor, musicians, drama teams, technical teams, and others to plan worship celebrations. The technical rehearsal at 2:30 on Saturday afternoon is my high-anxiety time of each week!

I don't have the traditional education of a seminarian. God gave me an alternative education by weaving together everything I've been soaking in since my conversion: playing keyboard in a band, leading church and community musicals, memorizing large amounts of Scripture, voracious reading, cultivating a curiosity about what makes people tick, and pursuing my passion to creatively connect people with their God-mission. My life doesn't make sense outside my God-mission.

"Mud and spit" is the metaphor for my life. That's what Jesus used to give sight to the blind. God has always used available, everyday things to do the work needed. I love God, and I want to be an available demonstration that inspires and gives hope to other people.

Truly, human reasoning would say this wouldn't work, but God's mission is beyond common sense.

As with Tammy and Kim, your life mission is bigger

than you. It's beyond your ability. You may say, "God, that's impossible because I'm not smart enough, I'm not skilled enough, I don't have the education required, and I've been divorced."

God has one answer to all these hesitations. God said to Moses, "I will be with you" (Exod. 3:12).

Moses then questions God about going to the pharaoh. "O my Lord, I have never been eloquent, neither in the past nor even now that you have spoken to your servant; but I am slow of speech and slow of tongue" (Exod. 4:10). In other words, Moses was a stutterer.

> *It is not what we can do for God; it is what God can do through you and me.*

God replies, "Who gives speech to mortals? Who makes them mute or deaf, seeing or blind? Is it not I, the LORD? Now go, and I will be with your mouth and teach you what you are to speak" (Exod. 4:11-12). In essence, "I will be your mouth. I'll take the ordinary and do something extraordinary."

Even when I mess up my words, God is there. You sense the presence of God. You hear the presence of God. You say it's got to be God because it can't be Michael Slaughter!

My Burning Bush Moment

How can I accomplish God's mission? "I will be with you" is all we need.

I began to become serious about this God thing during my senior year in high school. I began to think, "What can I do for God?" Later in my journey of faith, I've come to understand that it is not what we can do for God; it is what God can do through you and me.

My call literally came out of a bush when I was walking

around the corner of North College Hill High School. God showed me that I was going to lead these people out of darkness the Monday after the party. Every time I went past and saw that bush I'd remember, "There is my burning bush."

You and I, along with Moses, might say, "But suppose they do not believe me or listen to me, but say, 'The LORD did not appear to you' " (Exod. 4:1).

God's answer was to ask Moses, "What is that in your hand?" For the last forty years Moses had been a shepherd. So he answered God, "A staff" (Exod. 4:2). Every shepherd, including Moses, had a shepherd's crook. God took that ordinary tool that Moses didn't recognize as significant and told Moses to throw it to the ground. That was an act of faith. It became a snake. Moses went up against Egypt, the most powerful kingdom on earth at that time, with a stick and won! God takes the ordinary and makes it extraordinary.

Better Than You or Me

So here's the question we need to ask: What is God doing and how can I be a part of it? We need to be where God is moving. We need to act on what we know.

Jesus said, "As long as you have light, walk in the light before it becomes darkness" (paraphrase, John 12:35). This means that when we see a little glimpse of the light of God's truth, we need to take a step. To walk is to

We need to be where God is moving. We need to act on what we know.

act. Walk in that light before the window of opportunity closes and it becomes darkness.

Too many people hear a truth from God and instead of acting on it, they wait. When you wait, it may be too late. Take action, break ranks, risk the radical, attempt the impossible, decide to do one thing today based on what you know right now.

Life mission is bigger than me, it's beyond me, and it's better than me! God says to Moses, "So come, I will send you to Pharaoh to bring my people, the Israelites, out of Egypt" (Exod. 3:10).

Miracles Through You and Me

Miracles do not come *to* you; they come *through* you. Jesus affirmed this when he said, "Out of the believer's heart shall flow rivers of living water" (John 7:38).

> *Miracles do not come* **to** *you; they come* **through** *you. . . . Not . . . to help you* **be all you can be.** *They come* **through** *you to* **serve** *people.*

Jesus isn't limited to making you the best person you can be. He is saying, "If you follow me, you will become a source of refreshment and healing and creativity to everyone around you."

Miracles don't come to you to help *you* be all you can be. They come through you to *serve* people. The measure of life is what God gives through us to bless other people. God reminds us, "I am with you"; "I am your mouth"; "I am your resources"; "I am your strength"; "It is not what you can do for me, it is what I am going to do through you."

That's what it means to be a witness of Jesus Christ. The responsibility of witness is to tell and live the truth about what you have seen and experienced. You tell what you know, what's happening right now, what you're experiencing right now.

Your life purpose does not originate in how you imagine you; it's how God imagines you. That understanding leads to a God-sized life mission.

Begin that journey by walking in the light that you have received while you have that window of opportunity.

Discussion Questions

1. To whom could you say directly or pick up the phone and say, "I'm reading a book that challenges me to voice my mission in life. Would you be willing to help me by letting me try to describe my unique calling?" This is an ideal activity to do in a small group where a high degree of trust and care is present.

2. As you read this chapter, was there a moment when your heart raced and you said, "Here I am Lord, please send me"? If so, what do you need to do now, or who do you need to speak to before this day ends?

3. If you're meeting in a group, ask how you can pray for one another. Pray together.

Joining the Movement

 What could your entire church do to challenge and change the culture around you?

Example: What would be the most appropriate place for encouraging the people of your church to describe the dreams they believe they have received from God? You might ask your pastor if an upcoming message could use some illustrations along these lines. If so, then could you (or your group or team) write down a handful of "dream" stories—both visions that have come to pass and visions that are yet to happen. You might do likewise with a church bulletin board or newsletter.

Example: Does your church help people identify their spiritual gifts and passions? An appendix at the end of this book describes the materials that Ginghamsburg Church uses. How could you (or your group or team) give visibility to the idea of serving God by passion and gifting, rather than by simply "filling slots"?

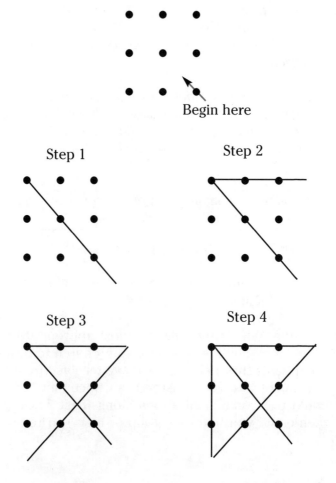

Begin here

Step 1

Step 2

Step 3

Step 4

Chapter Seven

Take the Plunge Right Here, Right Now

The Christian life is radical. It can't be simulated. It is not something you can ease into. It costs everything. When we say the word church *we usually refer to a building, not to a radical group of people who have been invaded by the presence of God. When we say* Jesus Christ, *we don't typically think about somebody who is radical. Instead we envision someone who is well-mannered and tame. Jesus was anything but tame, and he wasn't afraid to call a pile of manure just what it was.*

Which of the following boxes represent your picture of Jesus Christ? Check as many as apply.

☑ sometimes rude   ☑ gentle
☑ sometimes invasive   ☐ polite
☑ raises uncomfortable issues   ☐ patient
☑ talks a lot about money ☑ friendly
☑ expects an immediate response ☑ caring
☑ authoritative   ☐ safe to be with

How many did you choose from the first column? Jesus' interview with a tax collector named Zacchaeus *Luke 19* (zac-KEE-us) might lead you to choose every box in the first column. Jesus seems to violate all the etiquette of Jewish culture in his day. His approach is rude and invasive.

Zacchaeus was wealthy. He was also unpopular. Tax collectors in his country made their living by adding a sur-charge to everyone's tax. They were seen as traitors and cheats.

A point of tension frequently exists between those who would follow Jesus and those who are wealthy in this life.

Zacchaeus must have been a hard worker because being a tax collec-tor wasn't easy. Perhaps he was also a little uncom-fortable because Jesus was known to talk a lot about wealth. At least one-fourth of Jesus' teachings deal with wealth or pos-sessions.

Yet, at the same time, Zacchaeus wanted to see who Jesus was. Something in him needed to understand what Jesus was about.

A point of tension frequently exists between those who would follow Jesus and those who are wealthy in this life. Perhaps Zacchaeus needed a place where he wouldn't come into direct con-frontation with something that could potentially be costly to him, so he hid up in a tree.

As with a lot of successful people today, when Zacchaeus wanted to find out more about Jesus, he selected a safe vantage point.

As with a lot of success-ful people today, when Zacchaeus wanted to find out more about Jesus, he selected a safe vantage point. "He was trying to see who Jesus was, but on account of the crowd he could not, because he was short in stature. So he ran ahead and climbed a sycamore tree to see him, because he was going to pass that way. When Jesus came to the place, he looked up and said to him, 'Zacchaeus, hurry

and come down; for I must stay at your house today' "
(Luke 19:3-5).

Through the encounter that followed, Zacchaeus was
awakened to what it meant to be a follower of Jesus. Real
followers respond decisively to the claims of Christ.
Some people think they can follow yet never change, but
true followers know they can't stay in the middle.

Respond Immediately

What would you do if someone you had never met
came up to you and said, "Hey, come down here immediately. Today I must stay at your house"? This is a direc-
tive, not an invitation. It's a far cry from, "Hello,
Zacchaeus, my name is Jesus. How about doing lunch
sometime? Here's my business card; give me a call when
you have the time."

Is Jesus Leisurely?

The Jesus here is quite different from the institutional
"nice" Jesus that many people think about. One popular
song of yesteryear says, "Softly and tenderly Jesus is calling, calling for you and for me; see on the portals he's
waiting and watching, watching for you and for me." It
implies that a nice Jesus is happy to wait for you to
decide at your leisure to follow him.

That is not the way the real Jesus behaves when he
enters Zacchaeus's world. By the time their dialogue was
finished, Zacchaeus would say to Jesus, "Look, half of my
possessions, Lord, I will give to the poor; and if I have
defrauded anyone of anything, I will pay back four times
as much" (Luke 19:8). Actions like that suggest that
something radical has happened inside Zacchaeus's
soul.

Jesus responds, "Today salvation has come to this
house" (Luke 19:9). After all, that's why Jesus came to

earth: "For the Son of Man came to seek out and to save the lost" (Luke 19:10).

When Jesus called people, he often conveyed the idea of immediacy. Zacchaeus was in a tree because he thought it would keep him at a safe distance. Zacchaeus thought Jesus would simply walk by and make no demands on his life because he wouldn't notice Zacchaeus.

But Jesus looked up and said, "Zacchaeus, come down immediately."

It is significant that Zacchaeus refers to Jesus as Lord. Zacchaeus responded so quickly to Jesus because he recognized him as Lord, as the absolute authority of the cosmos.

> *Their message was: "No, Caesar isn't Lord. Jesus is Lord." That is why so many of them died in the Coliseum.*

The term *Lord* was reserved only for Caesar, the ruler of the Roman Empire. The customary greeting in Palestine at that time was "Caesar is Lord." You were acknowledging that Caesar held absolute authority. If you refused to voice this greeting, you found yourself at the Coliseum, and it wasn't to watch a football game.

Zacchaeus's experience was more the norm than the exception. Jesus' first followers believed emphatically that "there is salvation in no one else, for there is no other name under heaven given among mortals by which we must be saved" (Acts 4:12). These radical people "did not cease to teach and proclaim Jesus as the Messiah" (Acts 5:42)—the Savior of the world. Their message was: "No, Caesar isn't Lord. Jesus is Lord." That is why so many of them died in the Coliseum.

Is Jesus Watered Down?

Zacchaeus understood that the call of Christ demanded an immediate and decisive response, and so he came down immediately. Christianity then was not watered down like it is now.

The first followers likewise called for an immediate, radical decision. The message of their community was simple: they preached the power of the resurrected Jesus, whom God had made "both Lord and Messiah" (Acts 2:36). Their calls for a response all stem from the identity of who Jesus is. They used imperatives like "Repent"; "Turn away from other gods"; "Receive the Spirit"; "Be baptized"; and "Be ready for Christ's return."

To follow Jesus is to place yourself at the disposal of Jesus. A decisive, deliberate action is not something that you achieve by a drift.

Don't Delay

Remember as a kid the first time you ever went off the high diving board? (Or maybe you've watched the following scenario.) You'd walk out on the end of the board and gently peer down to the water. An instructor, lifeguard, parent, or friend would be cheering, "Jump! Jump!" But you didn't budge. Eventually you carefully walked back to the safe part of the diving board.

You now had a problem emerging, because of a line forming on the ladder. You either had to jump, or make your way through the crowd on the ladder.

When we face situations that have potential risk, unknown adventure, and unpleasantness, we stand up at the top of the diving board thinking, *Uh oh, I could end up doing a belly flop.* Failure hurts. We all know that from experience.

The Postponement Syndrome

Jesus likewise demands an immediate and decisive response. What do we humans typically do when we face a situation that involves risk, adventure, and potential for unpleasantness? We postpone it.

People today are much like a governor named Felix "who was rather well informed about" the movement of Christ (Acts 24:22). Since the apostle Paul, who wrote many books of the New Testament, was a guest in the jail near Felix's office, the governor "sent for Paul and heard him speak concerning faith in Christ Jesus. And as he discussed justice, self-control, and the coming judgment, Felix became frightened and said, 'Go away for the present; when I have an opportunity, I will send for you' " (Acts 24:24-25).

Felix was attracted to this movement, and he continued to call Paul to learn more. He would even bring in his wife to hear Paul. Paul would be very specific about the cost of following Jesus. Whenever it came time to make a life-changing decision, Felix became afraid. He told Paul to come back another time when it was more convenient.

How many of us say to God, "When I find it convenient"? We don't like to jump into commitment; we'd rather ease into it. We want to try it out for a while. We even want to know if we can simulate the experience.

Simulations Don't Work

I remember a Wednesday morning in July when the worship planning team (we call it the Design Team) was wrestling about what it means to be a real follower. We were struggling for an illustration that would communicate the idea of an immediate leap of faith.

We wanted an experience that said, "Hey, I can't go back because I've made this decision and my commitment is past the point of no return." We wondered if we should use diving boards, bungee jumping, or something like that.

Suddenly I turned to Kim Miller, the Creative Worship Director, and said, "Hey, Kim, you're forty-something. How about if you jump out of an airplane? TODAY!"

She said, "Me? I didn't even let my children go to the top of the jungle gym."

"Then you're just the right kind of candidate," I replied with a smile.

Suddenly I turned to Kim . . . and said, "Hey, Kim, you're forty-something. How about if you jump out of an airplane? TODAY!"

I asked a staff person to start phoning parachute places. "We have to get Kim up in the air to jump out of a plane today!" I said.

Our first finding was somewhere that simulated the parachute experience. Even terrified Kim agreed that you can't simulate jumping out of an airplane. "I have to have the fear of what it means to make the decision to jump," Kim agreed.

Besides, we decided, a simulation would convey the wrong signal. Many people who claim to be followers of Jesus Christ have simulated the Christian experience, but they have never jumped. Jesus didn't give Zacchaeus the option of convenience. Jesus said,

Following Jesus is a right-here, right-now issue, and it demands a decisive, immediate response.

"Come down immediately, for today I must stay at your house." Following Jesus is a right-here, right-now issue, and it demands a decisive, immediate response.

The Airplane Jump

About five o'clock that afternoon, Kim found herself in a tiny airplane, 13,000 feet in the air, preparing to parachute back to earth. "I kept wondering if I had lost my mind," she told everyone later.

We used video to record her jump and showed it during our weekend church services. We used the experience to demonstrate what a relationship with Jesus is about: having to make an immediate, decisive response.

"I had to make a choice, and people don't like having to make a choice," Kim explained to the congregation. "We like the easy choice to stay in the middle and believe. But Jesus says, 'Choose this day whom you are going to serve' and 'You cannot serve two masters.' We have to decide! Following Jesus is a radical commitment."

Kim took a minute and a half to free fall from 13,000 feet to 10,000 feet, and then five minutes to float from 10,000 feet to the ground. She said that the minute and a half was hard because at 13,000 feet there is not much oxygen. She said that she was cold and it was hard for her to breathe. She thought she might black out. She also said the wind hurt her ears.

"Kim," I asked, when we interviewed her during the weekend celebration, "Did you ever in that minute and a half think to youself, 'Can I climb back into that airplane?'"

When you jump, you can't turn back. You cannot simulate following Jesus.

Everyone in the congregation caught the point. When you jump, you can't turn back. You cannot simulate following Jesus.

You start going where Jesus is going, doing what Jesus is doing, and being what Jesus is being through you. You may die, you may go bankrupt, but you'll never know what it's like until you have jumped.

Give Complete Control to God

One of today's biggest addictions is the need to control. It's what the Bible calls sin. It's trying to be God when there is only one God. (And it's not me or you.) In contrast, God calls for an out-of-control discipleship. Following Jesus is the opposite of control. You have to leave your comfortable, predictable place. For Zacchaeus, the first God's-in-control step was to give half his possessions to help the poor, and give a fourfold restitution to anyone he had cheated.

The Integrity of God

The basis for making a commitment that strong is to have a solid relationship with the one you're following, and a confidence in the integrity of God's promises.

God is a God of promise. When God makes a promise, it always happens. God's covenants are unbreakable. For example, God says, "For the mountains may depart and the hills be removed, but my steadfast love shall not depart from you, and my covenant of peace shall not be removed, says the LORD, who has compassion on you" (Isa. 54:10). The word translated "steadfast love" *(hesed)* is unfailing, unconditional, and not up for renegotiation. The love that God has for you is not up for debate.

Jesus' apostles said the same thing, but with different words. "Who will separate us from the love of Christ? Will hardship, or distress, or persecution, or famine, or nakedness, or peril, or sword? . . . I am convinced that neither death, nor life, nor angels, nor rulers, nor things present, nor things to come, nor powers, nor height, nor depth, nor anything else in all creation, will be able to separate us from the love of God in Christ Jesus our Lord" (Rom. 8:35, 38-39).

For too many people today, promise seems open for renegotiation. In a lot of marriages, promise means, "I do,

I do, maybe." Prenuptial agreements and other conditions compromise the promise of the wedding vows.

In professional sports someone signs a long-term contract, then a year later he breaks it to get more money. That's because the contract had a loophole.

For too many people today, promise seems open for renegotiation. . . . That's because the contract had a loophole.

God is a God of promise, and God makes me a person of promise. When I fully give myself to the presence of Christ, when I fully take into myself the presence of Christ, I'm invaded by his presence and I have the ability to think his thoughts. When I give myself fully to the promise of God's presence, the Spirit of Jesus rules in my life. "So if anyone is in Christ, there is a new creation: everything old has passed away; see, everything has become new!" (2 Cor. 5:17).

When I'm invaded by God's presence, I can demonstrate God's actions. I literally take on the integrity of Jesus Christ. I am no longer limited to my own abilities to be a person of love and promise.

The Limits of Human Love

Why do people make promises and break them? Why does the divorce rate in our churches and pastoral homes now almost equal that of our culture? We meant what we said when we made those marriage-vow promises. What happened?

Human love is always dependent on feelings and desire—which are always changing. But spiritual love serves. True love comes from above. It is supernatural, and it acts out of the love of Christ. It serves Christ's purpose alone. Human love cannot even understand spiritual love.

People of promise have clear boundaries and a clear focus. Their loyalties are real clear because there is one God in their life, and if they are married, one spouse. If they are single, they are celibate in their singleness because they are clear about the authority of there being only one God in their life. There is one Body of Christ that they are connected to. I can be a person of promise because God is a God of promise. I can love because God loves me.

Do Discipleship in Community

As a true follower of Jesus, I am a person of promise, but I am nurtured in the community of promise. As I said in the opening of this book, Christianity is a unique faith because it is about the restoration of community. "Where two or three are gathered in my name, I am there among them," says Jesus (Matt. 18:20).

The movement of Christ is a movement of reconciliation. God is putting together a new community known as the Body of Christ. It's more about connections than attendance. To join, you don't attend so much as you connect. It's not even about *believing* in Jesus, so much as *being* in Jesus.

> *God is putting together a new community known as the Body of Christ. . . . To join, you don't attend so much as you connect.*

What makes my elbow a member of my body? Because it's connected. It's receiving instruction from the head and it's passing on that help to other members. My elbow is not free to decide if it's going to attend body meetings or not. The same is true of my toes. Each serves its own purpose, but only as long as it stays connected.

Spiritually, the only way I become a person of promise is to be connected. "Being in" Jesus means that I am in the middle of Christ's body—a faith community.

John Wesley, the founder of the Methodist movement, observed that people could quickly beome converted during an enthusiastic event. But they would just as quickly fall away if they were not connected to a small group that would hold them accountable for their promises. He understood the idea of covenant.

One barrier to commitment is that too many people are wasting away life in front of a television set. Jesus calls for his followers to get up and get connected to something other than a virtual lifestyle. Personal, do-it-all-yourself religion is bunk as far as the Bible is concerned. And ultimately it will evaporate.

Commitment to Christ is like a marriage vow. It's not a conditional agreement for as long as it feels good and I think it's working. Rather it's for better or for worse, for richer or poorer, in sickness and in health.

God's commitment that "I will never leave you nor forsake you" is not based on condition. It is not based on your success or failure. "Nothing can separate you from my love," says the Lord God.

What could keep you from opening yourself to be invaded by God's presence and boldly declare that the Spirit of Christ rules your life? "Because of who God is, I can be a person who will live in the middle of the community of promise." That reality should give you great hope.

Embrace all the presence that Jesus Christ has for you, all of Jesus Christ, all of God. Let God invade your very being. Live forever in Jesus' name—but make your decision now. Hey, what are you waiting for?

If you're ready to make the leap of faith as never before, why not use "A Radical Confession of Faith," by Len Sweet, as the prayer of your heart?

I am part of the Church of the Out-of-Control. I've given up my control to God. I've jumped off the fence; I've stepped over the line. I've pulled out all the stops; I'm holding nothing back. There's no turning back, looking around, slowing down, backing away, or shutting up.

It's a life against the odds, outside the box, over the wall, "Thy Will Be Done . . ." I'm done playing by the rules, whether it's Robert's Rules of Order or Miss Manner's Rules of Etiquette or Martha Stewart's Rules of Living or Merrill Lynch's Money-minding/Bottom-lining/Ladder-climbing Rules of America's Most Wanted.

I am not here to please the dominant culture. I live to please my Lord and Savior. My spiritual taste buds have graduated from fizz and froth to Fire and Ice. Don't give me that old-time religion. Don't give me that new-time religion. Give me that all-time religion that is as hard as rock and as soft as snow.

I've stopped trying to make life work, and started trying to make life sing. I'm finished with secondhand sensations; third-rate dreams; I can't be bought by any personalities or perks, positions or prizes.

I won't give up, though I will give in . . . to openness of mind, humbleness of heart, and generosity of spirit. When shorthanded and hard-pressed, I will never again simply hang in there.

I will stand in there; I will run in there; I will pray in there; I will sacrifice in there; I will endure in there—I will do everything in there but hang. I am organized religion's best friend and worst nightmare.

I won't back down, slow down, shut down, or let down until I'm preached out, teached out, healed out, hauled out of God's mission in the world entrusted to members of the Church of the Out-of-Control . . . to unbind the confined, whether they're the downtrodden or the upscale, the overlooked or the under-represented.

My fundamental identity is as a disciple of Jesus. And I won't walk through history simply "in His steps," but will seek to travel more deeply in God's Spirit.

Until God comes again or calls me home, you can find

me filling, not killing, time so that one day God will pick me out in the line-up of the ages as one of God's own. And then . . . it will be worth it all . . . to hear these words, the most precious words I can ever hear: "Well done, thou good and faithful . . . Out-of-Control Disciple."*

* Excerpted from Leonard Sweet, *A Cup of Coffee at the Soul Cafe* (Nashville: Abingdon Press, 1998), pp. 168-70. Used by permission of Leonard Sweet.

Discussion Questions

1. How do you feel about the prayer at the end of the chapter? Which lines most spoke to the language of your heart? Why?

2. In what ways is your involvement with church more like an "attendance" than the "connection" that Michael Slaughter speaks about?

3. Think about the parachuting illustration and the diving-board illustration. In what ways does each match your level of commitment to be a true follower of Jesus? In what ways have you tried to "ease" into a relationship with Jesus?

4. If you're meeting in a group, ask how you can pray for one another. Pray together.

Joining the Movement

 What could your entire church do to challenge and change the culture around you?

Example: Have you been party to a financial wrong-doing that you need to address? Does any organization in which you have decision-making authority need to "repent" like Zacchaeus did? Often you need the encouragement and help of others to follow through with the level of sacrifice that may be required.

Example: Has God led any people in your church to make a financial commitment similar to what Zacchaeus did? For instance, perhaps a businessperson declared bankruptcy, but later made it a point to over-pay each creditor. Maybe someone stole something, got right with God, and then went the second, third, and fourth mile to pay restitution. Stories like these are often hard to uncover, since most people are reticent to volunteer the information. But they often start a chain reaction.

Chapter Eight

Bigger Barns and Other Obstacles to Really Following

Our culture has confused us; acquiring has replaced enjoying. We think we find life in acquiring gifts from God rather than enjoying the presence of God. Jesus called it the bigger barn syndrome. We need to be able to enjoy the nice things that God gives us, but the gifts must not become rival gods who begin to drain life energy from us.

C an you identify with any of the following statements?

- "We should buy it. We could pay it off in just three years."
- "Check out this new image! That luxury car is going to make me look the part."
- "Can we afford to pass up this sale? Think of all the money we'll save!"
- "The stock market has been good to us. I almost don't mind the higher tax bracket."
- "What we really need is more room. Let's rent a self-storage unit for our extra stuff."

Before we know it, the Jesus life gets choked out by the "weeds" of abundance and multiple possessions. Whatever happened to simplicity?

We Don't Cope Well with so Much Stuff

Think over your past week. Did your life move in the direction of becoming more simple or more complicated? If you're in doubt, try to recall if you felt hurried, tired, stressed, or breathless. Do you have your answer?

We live in a culture of complexity. Life becomes more intricate through big houses, second mortgages, high-maintenance cars, ever-increasing taxes, revolving charge accounts, easy credit, multiple credit-card debts, lack of time to spend with our spouses or children, strained relationships with ex-spouses or stepfamilies, ailing parents, crazy in-laws, difficult bosses or obstinate employees (or both!), meetings that always go overtime, increasing amounts of junk E-mail, and ads that urge you to expect the winning Publisher's Clearing House number. (That rather limited list, by the way, came easily. I simply thought about my world, and that of the last person or two I talked with.)

Before we know it, the Jesus life gets choked out.

Having too much stuff makes life anything but simple. Like a telephone salesperson's bottom line, the emphasis is always on bigger, better, and more. The benefit of the latest book or gadget, we learn, is to help us do more, earn more, and possess more.

Instead of resisting, we give in. A week or a year later, we've become more tired, stressed, and breathless.

Today's culture feeds our passion to possess. It's the oppression of racing into a new millennium. But Jesus came to set free the oppressed, and that includes showing us values that lead to simple, focused living.

We've Lost Something Through "Recreational Shopping"

In recent years, Carolyn and I traveled to Myrtle Beach, South Carolina, with our son Jonathan's baseball team. At 7:30 on a Saturday morning, we headed out to Coastal Carolina University where he was to play. We had planned for a twenty-minute drive, figuring few others would be up that early. Instead, we sat in traffic for an hour and twenty minutes. The expressway had backed up because people hundreds of miles from their homes were going to the mall on Saturday morning!

Outlet malls seem to be one of Myrtle Beach's largest tourist attractions. Our experience there underscores how much our culture is into recreational shopping. Even beachgoers become shoppers when they give up a half day of sun in order to attend a time-share sales meeting and learn how to *buy* two weeks' worth of beach.

Acquiring has replaced enjoying. We have confused what life is all about.

> *Jesus came to set free the oppressed, and that includes showing us values that lead to simple, focused living.*

Life with Jesus offers a clear alternative. A lot of people follow a Jesus of their imagination, but when you encounter the resurrected Christ, the relationship changes the way you live. It alters the way you view possessions. As this chapter will show, real followers have learned the difference between the enjoyment of God and the enjoyment of God's gift.

Call It by Name: Greed

Jesus would label "recreational shopping" as the bigger-barn syndrome. He told a story about a businessman who was concerned about his investments. Jesus began his parable by saying, "The land of a rich man produced abundantly" (Luke 12:16).

We call the man's blessing a gift from God. Across North America, a lot of our "grounds" have produced a respectable crop. At many churches, we can look around and see that many folks have done pretty well with their barns.

We think life comes from acquiring the gifts of God rather than pursuing the presence of God.

At this point, our culture has become mixed up. The confusion is that we think life comes from acquiring the gifts of God rather than pursuing the presence of God. The wealthy businessman in Jesus' parable has been blessed, but he makes the same mistake.

Some people in my neighborhood think just like that. As my subdivision fills, developers keep extending it by adding more houses. Each new wave of homes seems to cost $100,000 more than the previous batch. During one of the construction blitzes, I pointed out to my children how quickly the new houses were selling. "Sure, Dad," they responded. "Most of them are our neighbors moving down the street into the new sections."

Like the farm owner in Jesus' story, we conclude, "God has blessed me so what I need to do is build bigger barns." We upgrade to nicer cars, build additional garages, buy storage sheds, and move to bigger houses. It seems natural to thank God for so generously supplying everything we need, and then we resolve that our next step should be to relax and enjoy ourselves.

God had some blunt words for the man in Jesus' story: " 'You fool! This very night your life is being demanded of you. And the things you have prepared, whose will they be?' So it is with those who store up treasures for themselves but are not rich toward God" (Luke 12:20-21).

Why such a harsh response? Because we miss the point entirely when we think that life consists of an abundance of possessions. "For life is more than food, and the body more than clothing" (Luke 12:23).

You have been blessed. Just the fact that you're able to read gives you advantages over the 1.4 billion illiterate people of this world. More likely, chances are that you're in the top 10 percent of the world's wealthiest persons, even if you're "only" a middle or lower-middle class North American. Probably you and I have had adequate food today, while thirty thousand children will starve before we go to bed tonight. Yet we are tempted to look at our abundance and be like that rich landowner who stored up treasure for himself but was not rich toward God. (See Luke 12:21.)

We are tempted... to be like that rich landowner who stored up treasure for himself but was not rich toward God.

How does a Christian become rich toward God? Jesus finishes his story with these words: "Sell your possessions, and give alms. Make purses for yourselves that do not wear out, an unfailing treasure in heaven, where no thief comes near and no moth destroys. For where your treasure is, there your heart will be also" (Luke 12:33-34).

Why is it hard to see life this way? Because we confuse happiness with greed. The issue goes back to the idea of coveting from the Ten Commandments. "Neither shall you covet your neighbor's wife. Neither shall you desire your neighbor's house, or field, or male or female slave, or ox, or donkey, or anything that belongs to your neighbor" (Deut. 5:21).

Jesus was just as blunt in his story of the barn-building farmer: "And he said to them, 'Take care! Be on your guard against all kinds of greed; for one's life does not consist in the abundance of possessions' " (Luke 12:15). In short: "Watch out. Be on your guard against all kinds of greed." Let's call greed what it is.

Commit to Simpler Living

Do you understand why life becomes so complex? Somehow we think we find life by acquiring God's gifts. That's not the right place to look. Life is not in the gifts from God; life is in the Giver. Life comes from God's hands.

There is nothing inherently wrong with these gifts. We need to be able to enjoy the nice things that God gives us, but these

Life is not in the gift from God; life is in the Giver.

gifts can become rival gods who begin to drain life from us. Confusion develops when we believe we find life from the gifts of God and when we focus on God's gifts rather than focusing on the Giver.

The good news is that when people encounter Christ, it alters their attitude toward their possessions. In other words, the Spirit frees you and me to live simply with a single focus.

Identify the Single Focus You Need

In the early church, "the whole group of those who believed were of one heart and soul" (Acts 4:32). I trace this to God saying, in effect, "When the Holy Spirit comes upon you, I will put my heart in you." You can have the heart of God when the Holy Spirit comes in you. "I will put my mind in you." You can have the mind of Jesus.

That focus does not square with the double-minded approaches of the day. Jesus said, "No one can serve two masters; for a slave will either hate the one and love the other, or be devoted to the one and despise the other. You cannot serve God and wealth" (Matt. 6:24).

You can't serve wealth and God. A lot of us think we can have it both ways. We live our lives such that every day we pursue the gifts of God. We accumulate the gifts of God, but we never find life.

Where do we find life? We miss it if our focus is in the gifts. Life is in the Giver!

Jesus wasn't rich. He was probably our equivalent of middle class because, as a carpenter, he was a skilled laborer. He constantly advocated for the poor. He hung out with rich folks at parties, but he didn't allow himself to be infected by the stinking thinking of his culture. As a matter of fact, he had a tendency to be hardest on rich people. He said, "Indeed, it is easier for a camel to go through the eye of a needle than for someone who is rich to enter the kingdom of God" (Luke 18:25).

When the Holy Spirit invades your life, you will be able to think and live like Jesus.

Jesus lived with a simple, single focus. Here's what he said was most important: "You shall love the Lord your God with all your heart, and with all your soul, and with all your mind, and with all your strength. The second is this, 'You shall love your neighbor as yourself.' There is no other commandment greater than these" (Mark 12:30-31).

A central teaching of the New Testament is that when the Holy Spirit invades your life, you will be able to think and live like Jesus. That means you are to love the Lord your God with all your heart and mind and soul, and to love your neighbor as yourself.

The Burger King ads tell us to "Have it your way," and Frank Sinatra crooned about doing things "my way." By contrast, Jesus said you can't serve God and yourself. Jesus' focus was to do only what God the Father does. "Jesus said to them, 'Very truly, I tell you, the Son can do nothing on his own, but only what he sees the Father doing; for whatever the Father does, the Son does likewise' " (John 5:19).

The same spirit of Jesus can set you and me free from the complexity of pursuing and acquiring all of this stuff. We can appreciate the good gifts that God gives us, but we can know that life is not in the gift, but in the Giver.

A businessperson came to my office and said, "Mike, something is not right. I believe in Jesus. I'm committed to Jesus. I'm successful. I don't owe any money on the two houses or the businesses I have, but I'm missing something. I don't want to reach age seventy-five and summarize my life by saying that I own sixteen stores."

Then he asked me a question. "Mike, you look like you are fulfilled. Are you really fulfilled?"

I said, "Yes."

"Are you missing anything?"

I said, "No."

"Well, why do I have this void, this hole?" he wanted to understand.

This man was hungry, and he was discovering that "things" can't fill his emptiness. People try to fill their hunger with food, sex, work, shopping, thrill addiction, and clothes, but they never gain the sense of being filled up. So they keep adding more toys, distractions, and possessions. In response, life keeps becoming more complex and complicated.

Use Time-tested Principles to Sharpen Your Focus

My grandmother died several years ago. There was nothing physically wrong with my grandfather, but he died six months after my grandmother's death. The day he passed away our daughter, Kristen, and I had gone to see him. She had wanted to say good-bye before heading back to college. He was dressed and sitting out in the hallway, glad to see us.

The only thing the doctor could identify as the cause of my grandfather's death was a terrible homesickness. I saw it in both my grandparents before they left this world.

A similar kind of homesickness is inside each person. We devote the best hours of each day to a focused pursuit in acquiring the gifts of God. In reality, our longing is not for the gifts of God. It's for a relationship with God. Intimacy. Something that cannot be met with food, television, sex, work, or shopping, no matter how many bigger houses and storage barns we build.

How can Christ's followers nurture the kind of single-mindedness that focuses on our relationship with God? Here are two ancient God-given principles that can be put to practice every week.

Principle #1: The Sabbath

The Sabbath principle deals with more than a day off. It is a day of re-creation not recreation. It is also a principle that God's people are constantly violating. "For in six days the LORD made heaven and earth, the sea, and all that is in them, but rested the seventh day; therefore the LORD blessed the sabbath day and consecrated it" (Exod. 20:11).

Our church campus sits in the middle of a 100-acre wheat field. The farmer who works the land plants, fertilizes, and harvests the wheat. Sometimes he leaves the field idle, because every farmer knows you must rest the soil on regular occasions. After baling the winter wheat, he could immediately plant again, but he doesn't because the soil needs a break. It needs to be re-energized for its created purpose.

When I was a kid my mom would say on Saturday nights, "Michael, you better go out to buy us some milk because tomorrow is Sunday and we can't buy milk anywhere."

I'd beg her, "Mom, don't make me go to church tomorrow."

She'd reply, "You need to remember who you are and whose you are." On the Sabbath we remember that we didn't make ourselves. Everything goes back to God to be made right by God.

You need to remember who you are and whose you are. On the Sabbath we remember that we didn't make ourselves.

On the Sabbath we also got together with extended family. We went over to my grandparents, my uncle came over, and it was a feast day. It was also dessert day. My grandmother would always make my favorite homemade cherry pie, and my uncle would turn the crank for homemade ice cream. By analogy, the Sabbath is a dessert day for the soul. It is the day when the fields of our soul are not being plowed up with our own agendas and ambitions.

The Sabbath, as a day of re-creation, enables us to re-prioritize our direction. Mozart used to say, "You can always tell good musicians by the way they play the rest." Do you know what's wrong with how we live today? We don't rest with the sense of re-creation. We are so busy that we never take time to deal with the inside stuff. We go through our weeks saying yes to things to which we should be saying no.

The purpose of the Sabbath is not so that we have more time to play golf! Instead, it's a day when we stop to hear

God. One Sunday I was in Myrtle Beach and I spent the morning walking up and down the beach. That day wasn't a Sabbath; it was recreation time. Instead I made Tuesday, the final day of my time off, my re-creation day. I spent the whole day listening to God, reading, thinking, and focusing, with the TV off and other distractions contained.

We put this Sabbath principle to work as a church. When our youth ministry was exploding with growth, the elders, leaders, and I took a retreat where we listened for God's voice. We came out of our busyness for twenty-four hours.

During that time we believe God said "Wait" to our idea of a larger sanctuary. Instead we have built a wonderful facility called "Planet Soul" for outreach to youth in the Dayton area. The 35,000 square feet houses game rooms, dance floors, a coffee bar, and a gymnasium. We built it believing that God wants to fill it with youth and children of this community. Just as 65 percent of our new adult members that year described themselves as being unchurched, we hope to target a similar high percentage of unchurched young people.

To put the new building in context, our facilities are located in a town of twenty-two homes. The biggest nearby city is Dayton, some fifteen miles south, with a population under 200,000. We are suburban or perhaps "open country," in the present day, but we recently considered it rural. Our facility used an outhouse for its bathroom facilities in the early 1950s.

If our strategy team had not stopped to listen, we would have gone forward with our plan and not God's purpose. We were willing to change our plans according to what we heard the Spirit say. Our human tendency is to make life increasingly complex; I'm not sure we would have sensed God's promptings if we had violated the Sabbath principle. This is the difference between being fruitful and being productive.

The Sabbath idea always brings me back to that place

of saying, "If I had one year to live, what would I do?" If that were my time window remaining in this life, I'd want to give myself to helping people become real followers of Jesus. More likely, I'd be in their faces, challenging them to new levels of discipleship.

Jesus said, "Take my yoke upon you, and learn from me; for I am gentle and humble in heart, and you will find rest for your souls" (Matt. 11:29). Through Jesus, simplicity is possible in the midst of our complex age.

Principle #2: Fasting

A second ancient principle is known as fasting. We refer to a downsized version of it when we eat breakfast, often our first meal in some twelve hours. This is the time we end (the "break") our time of going without food (our "fast"). Real fasting can be very difficult.

When I fast from eating it is usually for twenty-four hours. When lunchtime comes around and a Big Mac is on my mind, then I'm reminded that my real hunger is for the presence of God and not God's gifts.

In the Bible, the idea of fasting is often associated with food. In the Sermon on the Mount, Jesus said, "And whenever you fast, do not look dismal, like the hypocrites, for they disfigure their faces so as to show others that they are fasting. Truly I tell you, they have received their reward. But when you fast, put oil on your head and wash your face, so that your fasting may be seen not by others but by your Father who is in secret; and your Father who sees in secret will reward you" (Matt. 6:16-18). His point here is not to make fasting a superficial act that tries to earn points with God or people.

Fasting could also mean to take a break from TV—or shopping or work or anything else that shapes you. Fasting reveals the things that control us. When you fast you discover the things that have become a substitute for God in your life.

In 1971 I was a nineteen-year-old new Christian doing an outreach mission in Ocean City, New Jersey, with Campus Crusade for Christ. Each day I made it a point to come back to our base around the lunch hour because that's when the mail came. I was dating a woman named Carolyn White, who eventually moved from the White house to the Slaughter house. She wrote every day, and I would anticipate that letter. It didn't bother me to miss lunch because I would go to my room, ignore my roommates, and be alone with Carolyn's letter. I did not miss the lunch because her letters were feeding a hunger elsewhere in my soul.

Fasting reveals the things that control us.

The same motivation works with God's love letter. When we fast, the point is not simply to skip eating. We replace what we're giving up with the reminder of what we really hunger for: the presence of God, not God's gifts.

Food is a gift from God. It's nice, but it's not as good as the real thing.

I wear a wedding ring that cost $38. We bought it more than two decades ago when we were both students and that's all we could afford.

Carolyn once said to me, "Wouldn't you like to replace it with something nicer?"

I replied, "No, because I'm not in love with the ring." I look at the ring and I don't think of the ring. I think of the woman I love.

As you fast, read God's love letters and think of the God you love and who loves you. Let fasting help you with the homesickness that frantic activity or abundance of possessions can never fill. Fasting helps you find life in the enjoyment of God's presence, rather than in the pursuit of God's gifts.

You don't have to get caught up in it.

Real Followers Can Get There

"Weeds" in our lives tend to pop up at an alarming rate. We feel that we have so much to do, with so little time. We have people to see and places to go. Thousands of messages bombard us daily with suggestions of things we could possess. We hear constant appeals to buy it now and pay for it in three years, or five, or twenty.

Real followers can be like the seed that fell on good earth, according to one of Jesus' stories (see Luke 8:4-15). It grew without gravel or weeds. It was simple, focused, and free. And it produced a return that was one hundred times the original.

I want to be that kind of follower, one who finds far more value in God's presence than in God's gifts.

Discussion Questions

1. To what extent have you experienced the emptiness that this chapter describes, when acquiring has replaced enjoying? What alarm bells went off as you read this chapter, showing you ways acquiring has replaced enjoying in your life?

2. Describe a time in your spiritual journey when you hungered for God's presence far more than God's gifts. What circumstances led to that perspective in your life?

3. What has been your experience with the Sabbath and fasting as "focus sharpeners"? What other spiritual disciplines help you focus on the presence of God?

4. If you're meeting in a group, ask how you can pray for one another. Pray together.

Joining the Movement

 What could your entire church do to challenge and change the culture around you?

Example: What would a day look like that focused exclusively on God's presence? Often our prayers deal almost exclusively with things ("the gifts of God"). Try a twenty-four-hour period where you neither ask nor even thank God for anything. Instead focus on who God is, and your relationship with God. No go tell someone about it, and challenge that person to do likewise.

Example: Who do you know who has developed a simpler life through spiritual motives? How can you help tell that person's story as a model to others? Maybe try your church newsletter, even if only to make a suggestion to the editor that you've found a good story. Or maybe drop a note to your pastor (with your friend's permission), suggesting that your "downsized" friend might make a good sermon illustration.

Chapter Nine

Life Is Not About
Getting What *You* Want

You and I act as if our most important need is for safety and security. But real life does not come from getting what we want. Jesus did not choose worldly power and prestige over a cross. Instead, Jesus found his destiny by following God's mission.

One Sunday after church, I was impressed by two different images in my local newspaper.

One cluster of several pages focused on the Sudan in West Africa. The heart-wrenching photos and stories described 770,000 people on the verge of death from starvation. I hadn't previously even heard about the crisis.

The write-up contained very powerful images. One picture showed a woman crawling out of the high grass she used as a latrine because she lacked the strength to walk back to her home. I felt pain when I looked at her.

The same section of the *Dayton Daily News* included an ad for a BMW sedan. It appealed to the desire of today's luxury-conscious generation. It said: "For those whose mid-life is not a crisis. While owners of other cars try to regain their youth, BMW 7 series owners glide back the moonroof, ease back in the comfort of the plush leather seating, tune the 14-speaker stereo to the concert mode and thoroughly enjoy their maximum earning years."

What bothered me was that I'm far more aware of sedans than Sudan.

I'm well educated about BMW sedans. I even used to own a far more basic BMW. But I was living in an ignorant bliss about the pain and suffering of almost a million people who, like me, were created in God's image.

What is wrong with this series of pictures? We live in a culture of climbing; bigger, better, more. When I'm forty-something I should drive a nicer car than when I was twenty-something. I should also live in a bigger house. As a result, we know the BMW sedan well, but we have no idea that almost a million people are dying in the Sudan, or that thousands were being exterminated in the Kosovo holocaust.

What bothered me is that I'm far more aware of sedans than Sudan.

More than thirty thousand children will die today from hunger and starvation, and yet I'm numb. I'm indifferent. I do not feel enough of God's heart toward human beings. Instead, I'm allured by the comforts of the latest options on a BMW.

True followers need the mind of Christ. We need to align our thinking with God's thinking. We need to be jerked out of our ignorant bliss.

Seek Engagement, Not Escape

A growing commitment in my own life has been a movement from sedans to Sudan. If I'm following Jesus, then I'm moving. I'm not in the same place in the year 2000 as I was in 1999.

The tension between Sudan and sedan comes from wanting to be committed to God's purpose. God will create a dissatisfaction or holy discomfort. The work of the

Holy Spirit is to lead you and me to be fully engaged with the things that matter most to God. This is the opposite of indifference or casual interest. It means to be committed with everything I've got. The real follower understands total commitment to a God who wants "all of me."

Feel-Good Gods

Every culture has always had gods who support their thinking and lifestyle. I call them feel-good gods. Much that gets presented as Christianity really supports two self-centered values: personal peace and financial affluence. If you listen to certain television preachers and talk-show spiritual gurus, you'll mainly hear about a little fluff god whose primary goal is surrounded with making your life more comfortable.

Every culture has always had gods who support their thinking and lifestyle. I call them feel-good gods.

Those who accept Jesus Christ experience "the peace of God, which surpasses all understanding" (Phil. 4:7). But Jesus also brings tension into your life. He says, "Do not think that I have come to bring peace on earth; I have not come to bring peace, but a sword" (Matt. 10:34).

When I came to Christ, things were pretty good. I liked the way the world was going until Jesus came into my life. He brought and still brings displeasure about the way things are. As a result, I became engaged in God's dream about how things can be.

As God's people, we tend to reduce our commitment to little superficial acts. But talk is cheap. Words cost us nothing.

Notice God's dismay when people's concern went no farther than the equivalent of singing a song, saying a prayer, and wearing a "help the hungry" bracelet reminder:

Is such the fast that I choose, a day to humble oneself?
Is it to bow down the head like a bulrush,
   and to lie in sackcloth and ashes?
Will you call this a fast,
   a day acceptable to the LORD?
Is not this the fast that I choose:
      to loose the bonds of injustice,
      to undo the thongs of the yoke,
   to let the oppressed go free,
      and to break every yoke?
Is it not to share your bread with the hungry,
   and bring the homeless poor into your house;
when you see the naked, to cover them,
   and not to hide yourself from your own kin? (Isa. 58:5-7)

Taking God to the Streets

Instead, the gospel is a breakthrough. "For the kingdom of God depends not on talk but on power" (1 Cor. 4:20).

A relationship with Jesus is not about escape. It is a call to engagement.

When Jesus sends people into mission, he gives them his power to engage the evil in the world. He gives power to bring healing in other people's lives. "Then Jesus called the twelve together and gave them power and authority over all demons and to cure diseases, and he sent them out to proclaim the kingdom of God and to heal" (Luke 9:1-2).

Further, Jesus told them to travel light. He said to take nothing for the journey; no staff, no bag, no bread, no money, no extra tunic. Jesus didn't want his followers to be weighed down or distracted by "stuff." Passages like these make me wary of those who teach, "Let's talk about all the stuff God wants to give you."

Christianity is the only religion that is not about escape. Every other religion in the world is about tuning out, finding your center, or tuning into self.

Jesus is more interested in using you to engage the

needs of the world than he is in teaching you relaxation techniques! Jesus is about taking God to the street and meeting people where they are.

Showing Real Worship

True worship doesn't consist of coming together in groups, singing songs, having prayers, and processing a series of religious actions that we call liturgy. Instead, true worship is giving mercy and doing justice. As the prophet Micah says, "He has told you, O mortal, what is good; and what does the LORD require of you but to do justice, and to love *Every other religion in the world is about tuning out, finding your center, or tuning into self.* kindness, and to walk humbly with your God?" (Mic. 6:8).

In chapter 2 of this book, I described Jesus' picture of true spirituality. "I was hungry and you gave me food, I was thirsty and you gave me something to drink, I was a stranger and you welcomed me, I was naked and you gave me clothing, I was sick and you took care of me, I was in prison and you visited me. . . . Just as you did it to one of the least of these who are members of my family, you did it to me" (Matt. 25:35-36, 40).

The Bible's description of fasting is not simply an act of personal denial. "Oh, my stomach is growling; isn't God pleased!"

Instead, as the prophet Isaiah said, fasting is engagement. It is identification with the world's hunger—physical hunger, spiritual hunger, emotional hunger.

Notice the cause-and-effect relationship that Isaiah describes. "If you offer your food to the hungry and satisfy the needs of the afflicted, then your light shall rise in the darkness and your gloom be like the noonday. The

LORD will guide you continually, and satisfy your needs in parched places, and make your bones strong; and you shall be like a watered garden, like a spring of water, whose waters never fail" (Isa. 58:10-11).

You have power with God by your actions toward people, especially people in need. If you spend yourself on behalf of the hungry and satisfy the needs of the oppressed, then your light will rise in the darkness.

Don't Expect Life to Come Easy

Life isn't always easy, and the Jesus walk isn't about getting what you want. We want to skip the pain that comes from engagement in the world, but God doesn't deliver us from death. He resurrects us in it. God gives us life in the middle of pain.

> *God gives us life in the middle of pain. God doesn't deliver us from death. He resurrects us in it.*

We somehow expect that God is supposed to make life fair. Yet the greatest focus of the Gospels involves a person who never did wrong but is betrayed and deserted by friends in his greatest time of need. Then he was framed and cruelly punished by death. Worst of all, heaven was silent and didn't intervene until after Jesus was dead. From beginning to end, Jesus' life wasn't fair.

This is what Jesus told followers who had given up their job and reputations to follow him: "See, we are going up to Jerusalem, and the Son of Man will be handed over to the chief priests and the scribes, and they will condemn him to death; then they will hand him over to the Gentiles; they will mock him, and spit upon him, and flog him, and kill him; and after three days he will rise again" (Mark 10:33-34).

An Inconvenient Call from Randy

God does give life, however, through the discomforts of engagement with the world. The following is an actual dialogue that happened between our Worship Director, Kim Miller, and myself. Out of that initial discussion, we produced a video to tell the story, and we played that video, which is also scripted below, for the congregation. (Both are slightly edited.)

Mike S.: "I don't want to mention any names, but in my Tuesday night Bible study group, I noticed that Mike Porto, sitting in the back of the room, looked very tired."

Kim: "Yes. He looked like he had sleep on his mind. As it turns out, he and Tom Jelenek had been without sleep the night before."

Mike S.: "That would have been Monday night?"

Kim: "Right."

Mike S.: "But wouldn't each have been in his own home watching Monday Night Football?"

Kim: "Yes, they each started the game, but they got pre-empted. It seems that Tom has a friend named Randy. He met Randy about ten years ago while doing missions here at the church. Randy has called Tom several times since then, whenever he has a need. On Monday, Tom got an 'I have a need' phone call from Randy."

Mike S.: "Did this Randy really need help?"

Kim: "Yes."

Mike S.: "How did Mike Porto get involved?"

Kim: "Well, we weren't sure either, so we went over to Tom's house to try and find out more of the story from both of them." (Here the dialogue cut away to video.)

Tom:	"I was lying on the couch watching Barry Sanders and the Detroit Lions when I got this call from Randy saying he needed a ride to Peebles, Ohio. I thought, *Oh, no. The kids are in bed, everything is great, Barry Sanders is really starting to cook! It's 9:30 P.M.! Why now, Lord? Why are you doing this?* However, I told Randy okay and started to get ready to go. Then the thought came to me that it would be a long ride back if I would be by myself. So, that's when I called Mike."
Mike P.:	"My wife answered the phone and said Tom wanted me to go someplace with him. I was watching the game, too, and didn't want to go anyplace. Especially at 9:30 at night. But I told Tom I would go."
Tom:	"I picked up Mike and we then went over to get Randy."
Mike P.:	"Randy wasn't ready to go yet, so we helped him pack. By the time we hit the road, it was 11:00 P.M."
Tom:	"We asked Randy if he knew the way to Peebles, and he said we had to go until we hit Route 32, which was only about an hour away."
Mike P.:	"Well, we kept going and going and an hour later decided we had missed the road and were kind of lost. It was now midnight."
Tom:	"But we finally got back on track and eventually got close to Peebles. We found Randy a motel room and then started back home. It was now 2:00 A.M."
Mike P.:	"We finally got back home around 3:30 A.M. I really wasn't all that tired, either. It had been a great trip. I was wide awake until later when I got sleepy in Mike's Bible study group!"

Why would two grown men give up *Monday Night Football* on the spur of the moment?

Some people think that coming to church is what makes them faithful to God. No! You have power with God evidenced by your actions with people. Sometimes the problem is that too many people are awake for the church service and sleep while God is working during the week.

Tom and Mike didn't have to leave their comfort zones, driving to an unknown place into the wee hours of the morning. They did so because someone needed their help. They became engaged in a brother's problem and they didn't resort to escapism. They didn't take the easy route.

> *You have power with God, evidenced by your actions with people.*

Jesus once took three of his disciples—Peter, James, and John—to the top of a mountain, where they had quite a spiritual experience. Immediately they said, "Let's build shrines up here!" The three planned to stay up there forever. Escape! But Jesus said they couldn't stay on the mountain. (See Mark 9:2-10.)

Redirecting Your Passion

When you hear the word *miracle* perhaps you think of a blind person seeing, a deaf person hearing, or a tumor going away. The biggest miracle I know occurs when God causes a selfish person to lay down his or her life for the sake of love. Those other miracles usually don't change anyone other than the individual who experiences it. The bigger miracle, then, occurs when God changes a person's focus from the sedan to the Sudan.

Such changes don't come easily. Even Jesus spent a sleepless night, asking God if a "Plan B" were possible. Just before he was to be arrested, beaten, and nailed to a cross to die a painful death, Jesus prayed, " 'Father, if you are willing, remove this cup from me; yet, not my will but yours be done.' Then an angel from heaven

Jesus' life shows that passionate people lose sleep over life's mission.

appeared to him and gave him strength. In his anguish he prayed more earnestly, and his sweat became like great drops of blood falling down on the ground" (Luke 22:42-44).

Likewise, we ask, "Lord, do you have another destiny for me? Remove this situation. Grant me a life free from pain. Make my life safe and secure." When we have a sleepless night, we assume something is wrong. Jesus' life shows that passionate people lose sleep over life's mission.

If you think about the people who have influenced you

You can never know passionate living, the power of God's resurrection, without accepting the pain that goes with it.

most, such as a teacher, chances are they were people of passion. Likewise, business leaders I learn from tend to be passionate people. Passionate people compose symphonies. They design great buildings. They paint great paintings. They write great books. They solve human problems. They go beyond conformity. They give it everything they have.

Prepare for Blood, Sweat, and Tears

You can never know passionate living, the power of God's resurrection, without accepting the pain that goes with it. Making the commitment means doing life right, not easy. It may call for blood, sweat, and tears. Something bad comes into your life. Your boss tells you that you have been laid off. Your child rebels. The doctor tells you that the cancer is still present. You say, "Oh, Lord, if it is possible, remove this." Then, like Jesus, we say, "but thy will be done." It is what you want, God, not what I want.

Not What We Want

This is the most important question we can ask: What do you want, Lord? I know what I want. I want my kids to be healthy and successful. I want to make a nice living. I want to have a good marriage. I want to make a contribution in this world. I assume that my real need is for safety and security.

I know what I want. . . . I assume that my real need is for safety and security.

But that's not where passionate destiny comes from. The apostle Paul says passionate living comes from power through suffering, as we'll discuss further in chapter 11. "I want to know Christ and the power of his resurrection and the sharing of his sufferings by becoming like him in his death, if somehow I may attain the resurrection from the dead" (Phil. 3:10-11).

Jesus was God crucified for you and me. Jesus didn't run or quit. It's easy to say, "Yes, God," when you're gathered with 30, 300, or 3,000 people. For Jesus, everyone else bailed, and he was the only one standing. Yet he stuck with his purpose. "Jesus said to them, 'My food is to do the will of him who send me and to complete his work' " (John 4:34). That's true passion!

I sometimes deal with depression, grief, and frustration. Jesus experienced it all during his last week on earth, and he didn't even use his sense of being forsaken as an excuse to stop. He never forgot who he was and why he was here.

I regularly deal with doubt. God never takes doubt away. At least in my twenty-some years of being a follower of Jesus, he's never taken doubt away. He gives us faith in the midst of doubt.

Jesus did not give in to doubt, even as he fulfilled the ancient Scripture just before he died, calling out, "My God, my God, why have you forsaken me?" (Matt. 27:46; see also Psalm 22:1).

Jesus demonstrates ultimate passion. His death on the cross says that God would rather go to hell for you than go to heaven without you. That's total life commitment.

> **God would rather go to hell for you than go to heaven without you.**

Because we are created in the image of God, we too are wired for passion. We are made for total commitment. God wants all of you and me. A going-all-the-way resolve says I would do absolutely anything in order that the purpose of God would be fulfilled in me and through me:

- "I'll write the check tomorrow."
- "I'll get up an hour early to hear God's voice."
- "I'll work at a job for less money if that's God's plan for my life."
- "I'll go to counseling with my spouse."
- "Even if my spouse walks out, I'll do anything necessary so that God's way can be fulfilled through me."
- "I will stick to the plan even when God is silent. In this age of fruitless religion and lukewarm believers, I will live out of a sense of destiny."
- "I will keep on keeping on even when I don't hear the angel's voice."

Something Has to Die

Passion requires blood, sweat, and tears. It means all of me. It means everything. "In his anguish he prayed more earnestly, and his sweat became like great drops of blood falling down on the ground" (Luke 22:44). Why did Jesus have to die? Why couldn't God do it another way? Evil has filled the world that God created and loves. Neither police nor armies can get rid of evil. You can lock an evil person in a jail cell, and even put an evil person to death. But none of that does away with the dark impulses inside of everyone.

> *Evil has filled the world that God created and loves. . . . On the cross, evil was absorbed into Jesus' body like a sponge.*

On the cross, evil was absorbed into Jesus' body like a sponge. Jesus' sacrifice was the only way that the power of evil could be broken.

Real worship involves sacrifice; something has to die. The kingdom that Jesus is about leads to a cross, not a throne. So many of us hear, but so few of us do.

It's the one who does, the person of passion, who changes the world. The apostle Paul said, "I have been crucified with Christ . . . for if justification comes through the law, then Christ died for nothing" (Gal. 2:19-21).

Following Jesus is not about donations. It's about going beyond conformity to give everything I have to the one who gave me everything he is. Blood, sweat, and tears are not for wimps.

True worship involves sacrifice. Something has to die. It's people of passion who change the world, and that's who I want to be.

Discussion Questions

1. What wakes you up in the morning? Most days what do you most look forward to doing or becoming? In what ways would your answer define your "passion"?

2. How do you handle the "but it's not fair" situations that God seems to present in your life? What did you learn from this chapter about how you might respond?

3. In what ways is your life moving from a focus on things like a "sedan" to concerns like the "Sudan"?

4. If you're meeting in a group, ask how you can pray for one another. Pray together.

Joining the Movement

What could your entire church do to challenge and change the culture around you?

Example: What is your church doing, both locally and globally, to feed the poor and help the helpless in Jesus' name? What could you do next?

Example: How could you help expand your church's understanding of worship, so that it goes beyond what happens Sunday mornings only (or equivalent)? What initiative in your community could you champion that would live out the kind of worship described in this chapter?

Chapter Ten

Do Not
Try This Alone

God's reality checks remind us that we cannot control life. If you live your life passionately for Jesus Christ, only then will you truly live. Is this the kind of future to which you've said "yes"?

Dick Morris was a brilliant adviser to President Bill Clinton. Some people say Clinton wouldn't have made it to the White House if it weren't for this talented strategist.

Morris deceived his wife for twenty years about his sexual addiction and his relationships with other women. He thought that as long as he was successful in his professional life, he could do whatever he wanted in his private life. An increasing number of people have adopted this attitude today: "It doesn't matter who I am if I do my job well."

The very moment Clinton was giving his acceptance speech as the party nominee at the Democratic National Convention, Morris's pager went off. He looked at it and it read, "*Star* magazine." He decided to ignore it.

It beeped again. He looked down and it read, "Regarding Sharon Rowlands." She was one of the prostitutes he had visited.

He later said, "At that point, I knew my life was done."

Whatever was causing dysfunction in his private life came out in his professional life. He couldn't suppress it.

Control Issues

That's true with everyone. You may think you can hide your secret life, but ultimately it will find you out. Ultimately, you will self-destruct.

There is something harmful in you and me that desires to be in command of our tendency toward destruction (which we'll describe in the final chapter). We think we might be able to control it.

In the long run, however, we're powerless over this force. We crave the very thing that will take our life away. You may think you can hide pride, arrogance, selfish ambition, gossip, lust, anger, or other forces and addictions, but the power that causes our destruction is what we are strangely drawn toward.

> *In the long run, however, we're powerless over this force. We crave the very thing that will take our life away.*

The real issue is a broken piece, a dark side inside each person. It's what the Bible calls sin.

Sin is that part in you and me that wants to rebel against God's created order. It even convinces us that we can win against God.

Deep inside we know that we're not being who God created us to be. We want to be more. We want to live up to the values we know come from God. We want to go forward, but sometimes we try to do it alone.

Plan for a Reality Check

Jesus received a plea for help from one of the most "have arrived" people around. Jairus had everything someone of his time could have wanted. He had job security and a pension plan. He could afford the best doctors and medical specialists available. He was invited to all the right clubs. He could travel. His whole town knew him and looked up to him.

Then something happened that was totally out of Jairus's control.

Don't Be Surprised

Jairus's twelve-year-old daughter had become deathly ill. No matter how good he had it, he couldn't control this event. He was abruptly reminded that success and security are illusions because we all die, whether rich or poor. No one is immune or exempt.

That's why Jairus came to Jesus, "fell at his feet and begged him repeatedly, 'My little daughter is at the point of death. Come and lay your hands on her, so that she may be made well, and live' " (Mark 5:22-23).

Most people, whatever their station in life, have had or will have a reality check like that. Perhaps a situation has already happened in your life and you realize you are not in control. I had that in my own family when my dad called and said that the doctor had found a spot on his lung. All of a sudden, everything changes.

Look for Jesus

Where do you turn when you are in a situation that is beyond your competency? Jairus had heard about a teacher named Jesus. He didn't fully understand who Jesus was. (Even today, who can fully grasp what it means to be the Son of God?) He had heard enough, however, to know that Jesus had a reputation for making the impossible possible.

Jairus didn't care what anyone else thought, or whether they laughed. He submitted himself to Jesus and cried, in effect, "Help!"

The same thing happens today as people are looking for someone who can prove that no one or nothing is hopeless. As Easter reminds the world each year, it's not over till it's over—and even then, it's not really over.

Before Jesus reaches Jairus's home, word comes that the daughter has died. The messengers also say that all hope is gone. It's too late. God can't help now. God won't help now.

Jairus has taken a positive step of faith toward Jesus, and now the naysayers try to explain why the door is closed. In other settings they might have said: "You can't"; "You're not smart enough"; "You're not big enough"; "You're not rich enough"; "You're not pretty enough"; or any of a dozen other limiting conclusions.

Don't Be Afraid

Jesus' first words back to Jairus are to not be afraid. "Do not fear, only believe" (Mark 5:36). Fear causes us to live below our potential. It paralyzes us. It causes us not to take risks. When we try to live safe and calculated lives, we miss the great purpose for which we were made.

When we try to live safe and calculated lives, we miss the great purpose for which we were made.

Fear breaks down the trust we have with God. We may still acknowledge that God is all God claims to be, but we might not trust God enough to take action.

Fear also breaks down the trust we have with each other in relationships. We fear what people will think, "If I take a stand, step out, and do what I believe, someone might laugh at me," we rationalize.

People laughed at Jesus when he responded, "The

child is not dead but sleeping" (Mark 5:39). Fearing what people think, we shrink back into the background and do not live in the way God created us to live.

Jairus's daughter had physically died, but we can die in other ways. The worst kind of death is to be dead while you are still alive. Many people don't realize they're dead, especially when their bodies are still living! They are the same people they were this time last year, but they've quit growing. They have stopped becoming the person God has created them to be.

Doubt and fear limit our possibilities. When all we hear is the word *can't,* they prevent us from turning to the one who says, "But *I* can." That kind of faith and support is what God used to lead the Sampley family (see sidebar) to overcome major obstacles, including the tragic death of a child, to become church-supported missionaries.

Trust God

Jairus, like us, needed to watch who he was listening to. "Your daughter is dead; it's too late; you can't." These words lack hope or faith.

Listen to Belief

Orville and Wilbur Wright, sons of a pastor, grew up in the Dayton area about fifteen to twenty miles south of my congregation. They show what can happen when you don't listen to all the naysayers around you.

In 1903, at the very moment when they were flying their first plane, an astronomer named Simon Newcomb finished an article "proving" the impossibility of flight. Part of that article said: "There is no possible combination of known substances, known forms of machinery, and known forms of force that can be united in a practical machine by which men shall fly long distances through the air. It is impossible."

As a preacher, the father of the Wright brothers had a different philosophy. Over the years, as he saw his boys being limited to the routines of bicycle repair, he said, in effect, "I'll just tell them about the empty tomb and stand back and watch them fly." That's the "dynamic equivalent" version of Jesus' words to Jairus, "Don't be afraid."

Tom and Elaine Sampley: Real Followers Who Became Missionaries

In 1988 at age forty-five, Elaine and I sold our new home, left our congregation, and went to Bible college, together with a time of language study, culture training, and church planting experience. The Lord had opened the door for us to go to the Czech Republic to help plant churches there through TEAM (The Evangelical Alliance Mission).

God had used Mike Slaughter as a catalyst to challenge Elaine and me to give our lives to serve God with the talents he has given us, anywhere he would choose to use us. Mike calls it "radical abandonment to Jesus."

Our congregation has heavily supported us all along the way, both financially and in prayer. For example, we E-mail weekly with Ron Musilli, a longtime friend at church, whose home group has adopted us, sending us vitamins and other care packages.

God has been with us every step of the way as we broke out of our "comfort zone" of living in Tipp City and selling real estate. Only through the "be strong and courageous" commands of God (see Joshua 1:9) are we able to establish reproducing churches in the former "eastern bloc" country of Czechoslovakia.

Act on Faith

After telling Jairus not to fear, Jesus then said, "Just believe." The world says, "You've missed God's opportunity" and "The clock can't be reset." Divorce, prison, bankruptcy, and pink slips all want to tell us that we have no future, that life is beyond any control in that area.

Jesus' answer to each of these failed dreams is, "You're not dead, you're just sleeping."

Jesus sees nothing as dead or beyond hope. That's why a murderer who masterminded a genocide movement against the church could say, "I can do all things through him who strengthens me" (Phil. 4:13).

Jesus sees everyone in him as alive and full of possibilities. Jesus sees beyond the limits that you or anyone else has placed upon you. When I hear about or see others in a particular situation where it looks like the odds are against them, I remind myself of Philippians 4:13. "You serve a God who makes the impossible possible," I tell myself—and sometimes them too.

The world says, "You've missed God's opportunity" and "The clock can't be reset."... Jesus' answer to each of these failed dreams is, "You're not dead, you're just sleeping."

For the disciples sitting around feeling depressed after Jesus was crucified, Jesus walks through the wall and joins them. For the children of Israel who were headed to the promised land, God parts the seas so his people can walk through. Every problem in life has a God-given solution.

Helen Keller, for example, was blind and deaf. She had been labeled mentally retarded and placed in an institution. Fortunately a teacher saw that every problem has a God-given solution, and Helen Keller eventually became a person who inspired millions of people.

Jesus is the turn-around specialist, no matter what limitations you face that keep you from being the person God created you to be.

Be careful, however, what you look for. Most times we find what we expect. Moses was an eighty-year-old shepherd who took on Pharaoh and won! He trusted God for the impossible, and then he acted like he believed it.

Do you expect the unexpected? God is a God who makes the impossible possible. Jesus said if you have faith, it will happen.

Hang Around Easter-Thinking People

When Jesus went into Jairus's house and said, "The little girl is not dead, she's sleeping," people laughed at him. He threw the negative thinkers out of the room. "He allowed no one to follow him except Peter, James, and John" (Mark 5:37).

You need to expose yourself to people who will encourage you onward as Jesus would. I love Jesus' people who are encouragers, just like Jesus. He encouraged the little girl to get up. He invited Peter to step out of the boat. He summoned Zacchaeus to get out of the tree and become the person God created him to be. Jesus invited Lazarus out of his grave.

It's important to be part of a small group and faith community where people remind you of what the empty tomb is all about. If you aren't, you may be missing who God wants you to be.

Refuse to Give Up

On the Friday before Easter, the worst possible scenario happened, as far as Jesus' family and followers were concerned. Jesus died. The disciples hung their heads and went back to fishing. Three days later, the unexpected happened. Even death couldn't stop God's plan.

Some of the people reading this book may be in the last stages of life on this earth. Remember that even when it's over, it's not over. Refuse to give up. Tell yourself, "I am going to live my life passionately for Jesus Christ until I die, and then I'm going to live forever."

Always Reach for God's Son

I was created to fly and to rise above my limitations, but I can't do that alone. I'm not afraid to admit that I need help. I don't care who is looking or who laughs because I am going to reach to the only one who can help me.

The same is true for you. Even if you doubt, Jesus believes in you. God wants you to soar above the limitations that are keeping you down. He wants you to fly higher and soar farther.

Tell yourself, "I am going to live my life passionately for Jesus Christ until I die, and then I'm going to live forever."

Clark Miller, a highly involved follower of Christ at Ginghamsburg, recently drew an analogy to the idea of flying: "Growing up outside Washington, D.C., I used to watch the airplanes take off and fly overhead, and I would look up in the sky and think that I could fly like that, too," he says. "So as a child, I'd pin a towel to the corners of my shirt and I would run across the backyard toward a hill. I would jump off the hill as high and far as I could, hoping that the wind would catch me and that I would fly. But eventually I lost the wonder and the motivation because someone told me that people can't fly. So I quit trying."

Sometimes Christians quit trying too. Young children dream about the stars and then they play out their dreams. Somehow adults seem to settle for the easy life.

They don't need to. What keeps you from flying? Jesus' resurrection demonstrates that God can make you fly. Don't go it alone. Hang out with God's people and always reach for God's Son.

Discussion Questions

1. When did you first realize you had the "broken piece" that Michael Slaughter describes? What would be a specific example from your life of the "part in you and me where we like to rebel against God's created order. It even convinces us that we can win against God"?

2. When are you most tempted to "go it alone" with a Lone Ranger approach to handling life when it seems to be going out of control?

3. If there is any area of your life where you've been told you "can't fly," what would it be? What do you think God is showing you through this chapter?

4. If you're meeting in a group, ask how you can pray for one another. Pray together.

Joining the Movement

 What could your entire church do to challenge and change the culture around you?

Example: How does your church say "yes God can" most loudly and clearly? What could you do, perhaps through your small group (home group, team, class), to show others in your church or community that Jesus, "the repair specialist," has a reputation "for making the impossible possible"? That is, how could your reputation better communicate that "Jesus sees everyone in him as alive and full of possibilities"?

Example: Is there a small group in your church where members give pastoral care to one another? What would happen in that group if you had more contact with each other between meetings than you spent in your official meeting itself? Why not make a covenant that when each of you feels discouraged by an "I can't" obstacle, you'll call another member to receive encouragement? Doing so just may change the entire character of your group!

Chapter Eleven

Spirit Led,
Not Success Driven

Sometimes our goals are right, but our motivation is wrong because it's tied to ladder climbing. Jesus didn't say, "Invite me into your dreams and ambitions." He said, in essence, "Go with me into mine." If I am following Jesus, I have to exchange my wish lists for his.

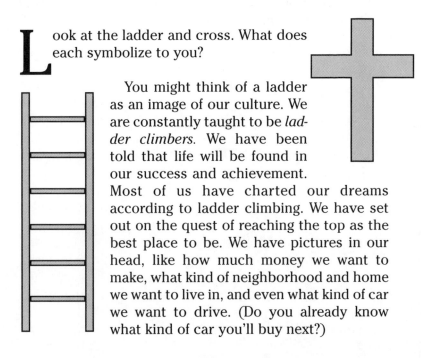

Look at the ladder and cross. What does each symbolize to you?

You might think of a ladder as an image of our culture. We are constantly taught to be *ladder climbers.* We have been told that life will be found in our success and achievement. Most of us have charted our dreams according to ladder climbing. We have set out on the quest of reaching the top as the best place to be. We have pictures in our head, like how much money we want to make, what kind of neighborhood and home we want to live in, and even what kind of car we want to drive. (Do you already know what kind of car you'll buy next?)

We spend a lot of time thinking about these pictures we keep in our mind. Then we use other mental measuring sticks to tell us how far we are, such as what kind of clubs and organizations we should belong to. Or perhaps we measure our success and achievement by our ability to go on an annual winter ski trip or on a beach trip every summer.

Right Goals but Wrong Reasons?

I'm not saying our goals are wrong. Sometimes it's our motivation that steers us wide of the mark. If we're looking for life and happiness through our material success and achievements, then we're headed for trouble.

That motivation issue affects every Christian, including pastors. When I came to Ginghamsburg Church in 1979, we were thirty-eighth in size in the Dayton North district of our denomination. According to my mental ladder of success and achievement, I thought to myself, *I have to be number one in the district, which means we should go ahead of First Church Sidney.* (They were number one with 600 people in average attendance.) Then, when we met that goal, I figured the next rung on the ladder was to become number one in the West Ohio Conference's 1,300-church listing. Even now, I know out of some 40,000 churches in The United Methodist Church system, we are in the top ten in size.

Sometimes our goals are right. I have no shame in wanting to influence as many people as possible in order to win the lost and set the oppressed free. However, I must also constantly check whether my motivation is wrong because it's tied to ladder climbing. Real followers can enter into a God-breathed life by being Spirit led, not success driven. This chapter will show you the challenges you need to face in order to live like a real follower of Christ.

Don't "Believe" Without Life Changes

As North Americans, we tend to develop busy, complicated, over-committed lifestyles. Then along comes
Jesus. We like him, we believe in him, we come to
church and sing about him, but nothing in our lifestyle really changes.

Sometimes our goals are right . . . but our motivation is wrong because it's tied to ladder climbing.

We tend to put Jesus in our pocket as another weapon in our arsenal to help us reach our stan-
dards of success and achievement. We pray things like,
"Lord, help me get that promotion." We haven't changed
anything, we're merely bringing Jesus along with us on
our quest to help us reach our goals, our dreams, and our
wish list.

The Plastic Jesus

Jesus said, "Follow me." Jesus did *not* say, "Invite me
into your life and bring me into *your* dreams and ambitions." He said, in essence, "Go with me into mine."

What does that look like? "If any want to become my
followers, let them deny themselves and take up their
cross daily and follow me. For those who want to save
their life will lose it, and those who lose their life for my sake will save it" (Luke 9:23-24).

Real followers do not behave like their surrounding culture.

To follow Jesus means I have to change my direction. I can believe and
bring the "plastic" Jesus with me, but to follow means I
have to go another way. Real followers do not behave like
their surrounding culture.

Sometimes Christians show more commitment to politics than to Jesus. Sometimes followers of Christ do a better job of following the almighty dollar than of following God's values. Sometimes we're more excited about dwelling in the temple of entertainment at the multiplex theater than in getting the temple of our bodies ready for a fresh encounter with Christ.

In many ways, if I'm following Jesus, I will be going a different way—on a migration in what many of my friends will think is the wrong direction. The concept of migration sometimes means an escape. I'm referring

If I am following Jesus, I have to exchange my dreams, ambitions, and wish lists for his.

instead to a direction of journey that some might consider a detour. If I am following Jesus, I have to exchange my dreams, ambitions, and wish lists for his.

Mannequin Spirituality

Jesus said, "Follow me." If that's the standard, how many people are truly following? I see a whole lot of *believers.* There are almost 400,000 churches across North America. The majority of those people in attendance would say, "I believe." But I wonder just how many are really *followers.*

What we Americans call the good life is described in the Bible as dry bones. One day as the prophet Ezekiel was passing through the desert, the Spirit of God led him to a valley of dry bones and said, "Ezekiel, what do you think? Can these bones live?"

"I don't know, God, you tell me."

"Here's the deal, Ezekiel; tell those bones that God will breathe and God will put flesh and muscle and skin on them. Tell them that God will make them live, and then they will know that I am the Lord. Oh, but Ezekiel, this isn't really about bones. This is about people who really aren't alive."

When Ezekiel went out into the desert and saw the dry bones, he asked God what they meant. He learned the dry bones were symbolic of how the people of God had lived and now were spiritually dead. At one time the people of God had living hopes and living dreams. Now they were spiritually dead and had worthless imaginings. They were ladder-climbing dreams.

So Ezekiel asked God what he should do. "O Lord GOD, you know," he said (Ezek. 37:3).

And God said to Ezekiel, "Prophesy to these bones" (Ezek. 37:4).

So Ezekiel prophesied to the bones. The bones came together and flesh came on them.

Previously, something had been standing there that looked and felt like the real thing, but something was missing. What was the problem? The bones lacked the presence of God. They lacked the movement of God.

That's what makes you and me uniquely human. It's not success and achievement, but our movement with the presence of God. We move by the wind of the Spirit. So, when you have something that looks good and looks like life even though it's not life, it's called a mannequin!

Stand Still and Wait for the Real Thing

My son, Jonathan, and I went to Florida's Disney World. One of the attractions is called the Hall of Presidents. All the presidents are on stage, but they're all robots. Disney is doing incredible things with animated models. They have real-life movements in the limbs.

Some attactions in the theme park take on even more lifelike characteristics through the use of holograms.

Those mannequins mimicked life, but they are not life. There's a difference.

I see a lot of the same thing in the church. Some people are mimicking the life of Christ, but it's not the life of Christ.

When you get into ladder climbing, a certain problem arises: You postpone life. You say to yourself, "After I pay my dues, I'll get to that certain level I desire. Then I'll have the time to be the husband I should be." Or, "When I get through this busy season, then I'll have the time to be the mother I should be." Or, "When I'm done with this project, then I'll have more time to give to the church and the mission of Jesus Christ." "When I retire, then I'll have more time to do what God wants me to

When we merely mimic life, we miss real life.

do." We're always postponing life. When we merely mimic life, we miss real life.

Bill Gauston was a professor at the University of Maryland in 1993 when he received the offer of a lifetime. The president of the United States asked him to be the deputy adviser on domestic policy. He became the adviser, doing what he loved to do. At the time he said, "This is what I was created for."

One day a letter came from his nine-year-old son. Ezra was telling him about his successes in baseball in the summer of 1994. He told his dad how he had hit his first home run. Then he concluded his letter with this sentence,

You find life when you're moving where God's breath is blowing.

"Dad, baseball's not fun when there is no one there to applaud you."

Bill Gauston went into the office of the president and resigned.

Christians go through similar experiences when they realize the breath of God is missing in their world. Real life is in the breath of God. You find life when you're moving where God's breath is blowing. We think we are speedboats, but we need to remember that we are sailboats created to move in the power of God's wind. We catch God's wind only if we stop and seek it.

Be Willing to Go Where Jesus Goes

"Wait for the God-breathed life." Those were the last words of Jesus (see Luke 24:49 and Acts 1:8). What do they mean to you? What are you hearing God say to you in this moment?

Life isn't about getting to the top of the ladder or about obtaining your goals or ambitions. Instead, life is found when you open your sails to the wind of God. Life is found when you go where Jesus is going. I emphasize *go*, not "stay" or "believe." Real followers are Spirit led, not success driven. Our busy complicated lives are *Real followers are Spirit led, not success driven.* too often an excuse for not following. We are overcommitted people. An overcommitment is really an undercommitment when it comes to your relationship with God. We say yes to far too many things. We don't consider that for every yes we say, we are also deciding no to something else.

An Unusual Gift from the Heavens

Back in 1973, a Wisconsin farmer was working out in his field when something fell out of the sky and landed in the next field. He went over to look at it.

The strange object was blue, almost diamond-looking, and frozen. He could not understand what he had found. Could this be some ancient glacier off the moon? Or from some distant part of the galaxy?

He was so excited that he called the sheriff and the geology department from a local college to come look at it. Everyone was stumped. All they knew was that it had a beautiful blue color and was frozen solid.

When it began to melt, however, it began to smell, so the farmer kept it in his freezer.

Eventually he figured out what it was. It was fluid that had been accidentally ejected from an airplane toilet.

The moral? Not every opportunity that falls into your lap is a gift from heaven! That promotion may not be the will of God. Every good thing is not necessarily a God thing.

Try the One-Year Rule

A lot of Americans are entering what I call the third stage in life—that's fifty to seventy-five years of age. It can be an incredible time. But job or financial security doesn't guarantee that you are going to find God-breathed life. First you must change your direction.

Other readers are younger. I hope you don't wait on the wisdom of older age before you figure out that you have to change your direction. You can change your direction now.

If you knew you had only one year to live, what would you do?

We need to begin to live by the one-year rule. Here's how it works. If you knew you had only one year to live, what would you do? That question can give you a lot of focus.

Time is a precious commodity. It is the only commodity we can't get more of. You can make more money and buy more toys, but no one can create more time. The one-year rule is a great tool to help you decide what you should do, and even more important, what you are not going to do.

Seek God Things, Not Good Things

We need to live life out of our passion. A recent *Wall Street Journal*–ABC News poll reported that more than half of all Americans would choose a new line of work if they had the chance. Over half of us!

You need to do what you really want to do. You need to live out of God's purpose for your life. A lot of good things are going to come along. People will ask you to get involved in community projects and other good things. You need to be able to separate the good things from the God things. Leave the good things for other people to do.

Instead, you need to move like a follower of Christ. True followers move with the wind of the Holy Spirit.

Here's another suggestion to help determine whether or not something is God's purpose for you. Resign from any organization whose meetings you dread. I began writing letters to those organizations in my life that I need to leave. They're good things, but I need to leave them. I am on some commitees with the vice presidents and CEOs of major corporations. I care what these people think of me. But I can't allow other people to define who I am and what I do. Followers move by the breath of God—God things, not good things.

Another suggestion is to ask this question: Will it further God's purpose? As a follower of Jesus, I am committed to going only where Jesus is going, doing only what Jesus is doing, being only who Jesus is being. So, if an activity is not going to further the purpose of God, then I am going to leave that for someone else to do.

Christianity must never be confused with a Junior

Achievement thing. Followers of Jesus give their lives only to the purpose of Jesus. There are a whole lot of good things that I have been involved in that will not further Jesus' purpose one bit. Those are not for me to do; I need to do the God thing.

Downsize—with God, sometimes less is more. Do you know how much of your energy goes into maintaining your stuff? When my kids are gone in a few years, it will be a condominium for me. No more cutting grass! Think about all of the things that our time, energy, and resources go into maintaining. Time is a limited, precious commodity. How much of your time goes into paying your debt? That new car that you want so badly—think about how many hours you will have to work to pay for it.

Carolyn and I have made a new commitment in our lives. We are not going to get anything unless we pay cash for it. We bought a used car, a 1987 Maxima, and we wrote a check for $2,500. It feels very good.

Grow in Community

In order to make countercultural choices like these, I need role models and heroes in my life. Gerry and Eddie Pass are third-stagers from Ginghamsburg Church (see sidebar). They made the decision to change directions.

Take careful note of what the Pass family did. They had a plan to get out of debt. They spent six months working nights besides their regular jobs to get out of debt. They downsized.

Then they followed their dream. They said, "We are really doing now with our lives what we have always wanted to do."

Consider this chapter as a wake-up call! Today is the first day of the rest of your life, what are you going to do with it? Whose ambition are you going to follow?

Eddie and Gerry Pass:
Real Followers Who Followed
Their Dream

Gerry: I started at my church as a greeter. I was already a follower of Christ when we came, but not a very good one.

Eddie: I started as a parking lot assistant, because I thought that would be a safe place. I became a follower of Christ a year later through the membership class. Then we got involved in a home group. A year or two later, one of the unpaid staff members asked us to train to become cell pastors. A few years after that we were asked to go to the next level—team pastors who support several cell pastors.

Gerry: In our fifth year at the church, I heard of a staff position at the church where I could use my administrative gifts. We realized to accept this role, we would have to get our finances in check. We prayed about it, and a second job came about for both of us. We worked the second job every evening for six months. Then we decided it would be a good idea to sell our home, which we did, and we moved into a condo. I took the job. I get up mornings and really want to come to work.

Eddie: Now I also work on staff at the church as a second job with the grounds crew.

Gerry: I can't believe we could handle the significant pay cut. We were barely making it before. We always had more expenses than income. Somehow God just makes it happen.

Eddie: It's been a step of faith that God has rewarded. We love every moment we can give to God through our church.

Application Project

Imagine you were going to follow the one-year rule. Write the following sentence on a blank piece of paper—or in a new word processing file: "If I had one year, what would I do and what would I not do?" After praying, write down your ideas. (My list began with the need to resign from several boards.) Then circle the one idea you're going to act upon first. Call a friend and talk about it. Now go and fulfill God's given purpose for your life.

Discussion Questions

1. *What has God gifted you to do to further the purpose of Jesus in the world? Be as specific as possible.*

2. *In what ways did the ladder-climbing image strike home with you? Why?*

3. *Which idea in this chapter made you most uncomfortable? Why?*

4. *If you're meeting in a group, pray for one another.*

Joining the Movement

 What could your entire church do to challenge and change the culture around you?

Example: At a New Year's service, a "Spring Cleaning," or other suitable churchwide event, you could ask several people to share how they've restructured their lives in order to follow the cross of Christ more than climb the ladder of success.

Example: Could you help develop a "Living More Simply" or "Downsizing for Jesus" class designed to help families be more ready to follow God?

Chapter Twelve

Are You Ready to Be Fully Honest with God?

Any time you allow inconsistency to exist on the inside, you cramp the connection between your spirit and Christ's spirit. Until you stop lying to God, you can never become who God created you to be. Instead, if Jesus Christ is really in control, he will use you to re-colonize planet Earth with a radical counterculture group of people who will embody the kingdom of God.

O n an out-of-town trip with my son's baseball team, I ate at a new restaurant. It followed a sports theme and included an arcade area with several virtual-reality games. I watched with amazement as one of the boys activated a snowboarding game. It was incredible. He stood on an actual snowboard, had the experience of a wild downhill run, but didn't have to take any of the real-life risks.

That's what virtual reality is all about. It exists in effect, but not in fact.

Be Honest About Virtual Christianity

The same thing happens in North American Christianity, in a stunning way. Pollsters tell us that approximately 90 percent of the population believe in God, and that eight out of ten Americans consider themselves to be a Christian. If 80 or more percent of this continent has surrendered its life to Jesus, inviting him to control their values and behavior, then why is the evidence so rampant of a breakdown in people's relationship to God, such as injustice, hatred, greed, violence, and indifference to people in need?

Instead, most people have come to associate the word *Christian* with something that could more accurately be called *virtual Christianity.* It exists in effect, but not in fact.

Real followers of God know firsthand the difference between the two. They've been in the presence of God and they've become honest with God

> **Virtual Christianity . . . exists in effect, but not in fact.**

about where they're a pretender. Real followers bring themselves to the place where they expose the pretender, because there is some pretender in all of us. "Truthtelling" helps us grow out of being the pretender.

The pretender idea is not a newly discovered concept for we seem to have an ongoing infatuation with appearance and impressions. Pretenders have been present since the very first days of the church.

There once was a man named Ananias (an-ah-NYE-us) who claimed to be a real follower, but in reality was a pretender. Ana-

> **Real followers . . . expose the pretender, because there is some pretender in all of us.**

nias owned some land, sold it, and "with his wife's knowledge, he kept back some of the proceeds, and brought only a part and laid it at the apostles' feet" (Acts 5:2). He announced that he was giving the church the entire proceeds of the sale. His wife, Sapphira (su-FIRE-ah), was in on the deception.

The apostle Peter confronted him. Peter challenged him about pulling a trick like this. "Ananias, why has

Satan filled your heart to lie to the Holy Spirit . . . ? How is it that you have contrived this deed in your heart? You did not lie to us but to God!" (Acts 5:3-4). Peter affirmed that Ananias was under no obligation to donate the entire amount to the church.

Ananias, having heard those words, fell down dead. As you can imagine, an awe of God came over everyone present. The young men of the church came in, wrapped up the dead body, carried him out, and buried him.

About three hours later his wife, Sapphira came in, having no knowledge of what had happened to Ananias. Peter named the amount Ananias had brought. He asked if it represented the entire price that they had received for the field.

Sapphira, like her husband, wanted to appear like a real follower. So she agreed. "Yes, that was the price" (Acts 5:8). Peter responded, "How is it that you have agreed together to put the Spirit of the Lord to the test?" (Acts 5:9). No sooner had those words come out of his mouth than Sapphira fell down dead. The young men carried her out and buried her next to her husband.

God can easily pick out a pretender.

As word got around, the whole church and community developed a deep respect for God. They now knew that God could not be trifled with. They also knew that God can easily pick out a pretender.

It is possible, by the workings of the Holy Spirit, to expose and move beyond the pretender in each of us. The first steps occur as we understand more about Jesus' purpose—why he came to earth, and how he wants to change us.

You Can Be Restored

When Jesus taught, people were amazed. "When Jesus had finished saying these things, the crowds were astounded at his teaching, for he taught them as one having authority, and not as their scribes" (Matt. 7:28-29).

Why? They noticed that Jesus didn't come across like other teachers. The difference was more than a matter of the confident way he talked about spiritual truths.

Instead, what Jesus said happened. Jesus' private world matched his public life. His actions and his thoughts were one with his belief system. When he said, "I am the good shepherd" (John 10:11, 14) or "I am the bread of life" (John 6:35), he became those "I am" statements. He was congruent. He had integrity of character.

I love the claims Jesus made. "I always do what is pleasing to [God]" (John 8:29). Can you or I make that claim? Jesus' private self and public self were one. He did not live in a world of virtual reality or virtual spirituality.

> *Jesus' private world matched his public life.*

Most of us lack that consistency between outward and inward. We tend to work harder at appearance. We fear that other people will find us out for who we "really" are inside.

When the spirit of Jesus enters your life, he restores the image of God in you. As a result, your private self and your public self become one.

This restoration is important to God. We're created to be like God, but because of our brokenness, we don't think like God thinks or act like God would act. God is really different from you and me. God is set apart from us. That's the idea behind the word *holy;* God is holy and we're not. But he wants us to be holy as well. "Be holy, for I am holy" (1 Pet. 1:16).

A holy person is the same on the outside as on the inside. Holiness means to be integrated, to be congruent, to be wholly consistent, to have absolute integrity. To be one thing, set apart for God, both inside and outside. This happens as the image of God is restored in a human being. Our consciences can become clean, and we can know an inner peace that passes all understanding. (See Phil. 4:7; 1 Tim. 1:5.)

You Can Be Reconciled

A second purpose of Jesus' ministry was to reconcile people with God. The Bible makes an incredible statement. It says, "There is . . . no one who seeks God" (Rom. 3:11 NIV).

God created you and me. God is the author of life. God holds life together. God sustains us. You would think people would move toward God in order to find life. Somehow, we don't.

If not one human being is truly trying to find God, then what are we seeking? We give ourselves to self-consumption rather than self-giving. Jesus came to turn us from self to God and from getting to giving in order that we may know real life, not virtual reality. Some people even look to religion and church, trying to get God to do magic in their life so they'll be "realized."

> *Jesus came to turn us from self to God and from getting to giving . . . from self-realization to God-realization.*

Instead, Jesus came to turn us from self-realization to God-realization. "And you, who once were estranged and hostile in mind, doing evil deeds, he has now reconciled in his body of flesh by his death, in order to present you holy and blameless and irreproachable before him" (Col. 1:21-22 RSV).

Jesus came not only to reconcile us to God, but to reunite us with each other. "Be reconciled to your brother," Jesus taught in the Sermon on the Mount (Matt. 5:24 RSV). "God, who reconciled us to himself through Christ . . . has given us the ministry of reconciliation" (2 Cor. 5:18).

At my congregation we want to set the pace for overcoming obstacles between people. For example, we believe God wants us to make a powerful statement about racial reconciliation. Our town, Tipp City, is almost 100 percent lily-white. Yet the church exists to be on earth what God imagines in heaven. So we are building a racially integrated church staff and doing ministry in places that enable us to build friendships across races. We are committed to racial reconciliation in this church.

Our town . . . is almost 100 percent lily-white. Yet the church exists to be on earth what God imagines in heaven.

One of the visions I had for our congregation was a church that would be racially inclusive. Ginghamsburg would be a racially inclusive congregation and staff, even in predominantly white Tipp City. By the late 1990s, that dream took major steps toward becoming a reality.

Pre-Christians should be able to look at the people of the church and see what it's like when Jesus Christ is really in control.

You Can Model a New Community

Jesus' ministry did not stop with the transformation of individual hearts and lives. His mandate is to establish a new community of people on planet Earth. His

---

Walter George: A Real Follower Who Became a Mentor

I'm a banker who was encouraged to live out my faith, not on a finance committee, but by going into the projects in downtown Dayton and building a relationship through the church's Clubhouse ministry, where kids in Dayton's poorest neighborhood receive tutoring, guidance, and love. Clubhouse is a project of Dream Builders, a nonprofit organization started by our church.

I get together regularly with Daniel Wallace, who was ten years old when we first met. We talk about his concerns, including his academic life. He tells me about the small group he leads at Clubhouse. They work on Bible verses and he gives them a challenge. It's something he might never have done without Clubhouse.

Daniel's mom, Tammy Wallace, was unchurched. A single mom with four kids, she is now making a big difference in her community, working tirelessly for the Clubhouse.

This is not a short-term investment. It's something you stay in for the long haul. It took two years just for the friendship to cement. I've needed to open myself to Danny.

Daniel is talking with God. He seems more at peace with himself and his family. My investment in Daniel's life has also made me a better person, knowing that I'm making a difference in one young man's life, bringing Jesus into his life, and keeping Jesus in his life.

---

church is to re-colonize the planet with a radical, counterculture group of people who would model the kingdom of God.

In other words, pre-Christians should be able to look at

the people of the church and see what it's like when Jesus Christ is really in control. These people will be demonstrating the radical unconditional love of God. They will model a community that lives out of God-realization.

But You Can Also Be Tempted Away

On each of these matters, you and I can be tempted to turn the purpose of God into virtual discipleship. It's the same idea as virtual Christianity: it exists in effect, but not in fact. "Let's not really do this thing," we say. "Let's pretend," or "Let's modify it a bit."

Human beings have an incredible ability to fashion gods in our own image. We're created in the image of God, but we reverse the equation. Instead, we construct gods who will serve our purpose.

The July-August 1998 *Utne Reader* contains a feature article called "Designer God." The subtitle reads, "In a mix-and-match world, why not create your own religion?" Here's the rub: The author is serious! His core idea is that we can have a god our way without any of the risks or costs. Yet at the same time, we can structure our god to appear on the outside like we're the real deal.

You think we don't do that? Look at what tripped up Ananias, whose story is summarized earlier in this chapter. He and his wife were part of a community called the church that had turned away from self-focus and self-consumption. Instead, church people practiced self-giving from the heart.

This church was living out the kingdom of God on planet Earth. "There was not a needy person among them, for as many as owned lands or houses sold them and brought the proceeds of what was sold. They laid it at the apostles' feet, and it was distributed to each as any had need" (Acts 4:34-35). Because this community of God didn't consume all they produced, they used it for meeting the needs of people on the outside.

One of their members was Barnabas. "For he was a good man, full of the Holy Spirit and of faith" (Acts 11:24), and later to be known as an apostle. Early in the life of the church Barnabas "sold a field that belonged to him, then brought the money, and laid it at the apostles' feet" (Acts 4:37).

Imagine Ananias saying to his wife, "Would you look at Barnabas? Everybody's paying attention to him now. I know him; we went to high school together. He's really got his life together. I must admit, he's made some positive changes. Barnabas took a piece of his property, sold it, and gave all the proceeds to take care of needy people. I want to be like Barnabas, but I don't want to pay that great of a price."

Ananias's desire—the power of God and the benefits of the community without paying the cost—was for nothing short of virtual discipleship. Ananias, looking at how God was changing lives in the church, was attracted to what God was doing. He wanted to hang out with these people without the accompanying sacrifice.

Ananias's sin was that of presenting himself to be one thing on the outside but being something else on the inside.

His solution? "I want prestige and privilege without price, so let's pretend." Virtual discipleship was born in his heart. Donation without sacrifice equals effect without the fact.

As Peter affirmed, the property-sale proceeds were his to give. Ananias's sin was not that he didn't give the whole thing. Ananias's sin was that of presenting himself to be one thing on the outside but being something else on the inside.

Begin Here for the "Real Deal"

This idea of heavy costs didn't start with the early church. It came from Jesus. At the core of the gospel is the message that it costs something to be a follower of Jesus. This idea doesn't rest easy with anyone, but Jesus modeled it constantly and taught it frequently. "He called the crowd with his disciples, and said to them, 'If any want to become my followers, let them deny themselves and take up their cross and follow me. For those who want to save their life will lose it, and those who lose their life for my sake, and for the sake of the gospel, will save it" (Mark 8:34-35).

I become concerned when churches, including my own, grow bigger. I don't want growth that leaves people unchanged.

Those who want to save their life could be described as on a journey toward self-realization. Ultimately they lose. But those who lose their life for Jesus' sake experience God-realization, and they ultimately save their life.

When Jesus said things like that, the big crowds around him suddenly become smaller. I become concerned when churches, including my own, grow bigger. I don't want growth that leaves people unchanged—virtual followers who exist in effect, but not in fact. I want us to be the real deal—real followers of Jesus. I want to lead us away from self-realization and toward God-realization.

Americans don't need to trust God . . . because we have credit cards.

I'm a baby boomer, and Jesus' call to deny myself is not

in my vocabulary. I hate the word *deny!* We're the have-it-now, shop-till-you-drop generation. My generation invented the Home Shopping Network. Americans don't need to trust God for the future because we have credit cards. Let's be honest; this is a hard saying!

Here's reality, though. When Jesus taught, "Let them deny themselves, take up their cross and follow me," he wasn't talking about a necklace or a nice piece of jewelry.

The apostles echoed that same message. Paul, for example, voiced this goal: "I want to know Christ and the power of his resurrection and the sharing of his sufferings by becoming like him in his death" (Phil. 3:10).

We can go for knowing Christ and the power of resurrection. Suppose your husband is dealing with cancer. Don't you want to see the power of Christ in his life? Perhaps a relationship has been torn apart, and it's dead or dying. You and I are eager for God's power to bring things back to life.

The second part of the equation is harder to sign up for. "Share his sufferings"? Become "like him in death"? Who wants that? "This Jesus needs a public relations person to work with him," you might say.

The Distraction of Appearance

Now the temptation sets in. "Let's modify this one a little bit. Let's give the appearance of doing what's right. No one will ever know."

If you've got two lives going on, that's virtual discipleship.

I turn on the TV and see some of these Christian shows talk about "accept Jesus and get rich." I want the gold Mercedes without any sacrifice, don't you? Where is the fellowship of suffering in this picture? The preacher left that out.

If you've got two lives going on, that's virtual discipleship. The treasuring of appearance to the point of losing integrity means I'm one thing on the outside but another on the inside. This tendency shows up far more than with certain television preachers.

Suppose a Christian reading this chapter is involved in an affair—or desperately wants to be! You may feel like a victim. "I'm a Christian but my spouse doesn't understand me, so I need another person," you say.

Another Christian is abusing alcohol or drugs. "Me and God have this little thing going on the side, but I need the fix for my nerves," you say.

Another Christian has a terrible conscience because of business practices that cheat people right and left. But you cover it up with an outward show of generosity at home or church.

Another Christian reading these words is full of hatred toward a former spouse, relative, or business associate. Yet you're so focused on looking good that most people would never guess what rages inside.

Another Christian uses E-mail to reach out to people in need. No one except you (and God) knows that the Internet is also your place of addiction to pornography.

You begin to die in your spirit as the distance grows between what you know to be true and how you live.

I got a letter from a friend who is part of our congregation. He asked what was wrong with having sex with his girlfriend. I explained that our God is a God of covenant and commitment. You cannot have the benefits of the relationship without the cost. We think we can, but that's called virtual relationships. Existence in effect without the fact is the reason our world is so full of broken people.

Living in Fear, Beginning to Die

We live in a world of virtual discipleship. Many of us live in fear. You may be afraid of being found out for who you are. The fear factor can build up to be quite intense. It's easy to expend a lot of energy in keeping up this appearance.

You begin to die in your spirit as the distance grows between what you know to be true and how you live. The greater the distance, the greater the turmoil and the greater the energy drain.

You notice that you start becoming callous inside. You sense a growing indifference toward God. It is too hard to get out of bed in the morning to pray because you are becoming resistant to prayer. Sleep feels better because your spirit is dying.

You become bored in spiritual environments. You sit next to your spouse in church every week and as soon as the emphasis shifts to spiritual truth, you nod off. You can't help it because of the atrophy of your spirit.

The most exciting thing in your life becomes your golf game, a stiff drink, or a secret fantasy.

You try to fill this void with mindless activity and noise. There are hundreds of ways to stuff the hollowness of a lifeless spirit with the pursuit of success and possessions.

You resist being still because stillness exposes who you really are—someone with no substance underneath. The most exciting thing in your life becomes your golf game, a stiff drink, or a secret fantasy.

You accept a world of counterfeit delusions, affairs, addictions, and materialism. Over time you develop a critical spirit.

Then you lead others in your downward spiral. Remember what Ananias did? "With his wife's knowledge, he kept back some of the proceeds" (Acts 5:2). You affect those people closest to you.

When I compromise, I damage Carolyn's spirit. I can even create spiritual death in my family through the unhealthy fruits of virtual Christianity.

North America has birthed a whole generation of children who have grown up without the knowledge of God or the fear of God. If you're under age thirty, chances are one in three that you grew up with only one of your parents at home. If you're under twenty, chances are almost one in two of the same. When you compromise, you not only wound your own soul, but you tend to hurt those you love most.

Why did God choose to deal so forcefully with Ananias and Sapphira? Perhaps God wanted to give a wake-up call to this new baby church. No doubt each of them already knew the temptation to shift to virtual Christianity. Maybe they needed to see that when they allow contradiction to

When you stop being an imposter, only then can you become the person God created you to be.

exist inside, they will die—either physically or as death of the spirit sets in.

As terrible as these consequences seem, something else also happens when you maintain a spit-and-polish veneer while at the same time you're really something else. "No one will know," you say. Yes, someone knows. You're really lying to God.

When you cut off God, you are no longer set apart for him. You lack the holiness, the congruence, the integrity that was yours to receive from God. When contradiction lives unchallenged inside, you literally clamp the umbilical cord between your spirit and Christ's spirit.

When you stop being an imposter, only then can you become the person God created you to be. Until then, you can't live life; all you can do is simulate it.

Remove the Lie Underneath

You're reading this book because you want to become a real follower. Genuine change begins as you become honest with God.

"Father, separate me from the pretender who's deep down inside. Amen."

I've pressed hard on this issue because a degree of pretender exists in each of us. It is important to ask yourself where you have been lying. Where have the appearances seemed solid, but you have remained inconsistent on the inside? Where has God searched your heart and said to you, with the apostle Paul, "Do not be conformed to this world, but be transformed by the renewing of your minds" (Rom. 12:2)?

Be Honest in Prayer

Are you ready to admit that God knows more about you than you could ever hope to know about yourself? To be honest means to agree that laughing on the outside while crying on the inside is merely pretending. Why not pray aloud the following prayer?

God, please search my heart (or if you're with a friend, or in a group, *our hearts*). *Lord, I want to be honest. I pretend a lot, wanting to be safe, to fit in, to be accepted, and to be liked. I confess that I have wanted to preserve my image at the cost of whole-heartedly following you. I have remained silent in the presence of falsehoods out of fear of rejection. I con-*

fess that many of my actions are motivated by trying to live up to the expectations of others or by my own stubborn determination to build a life without you.

I don't want virtual Christianity—existing in effect but not in fact. I come now to ask you to fill the voids in my life with the spirit of Jesus, so that I can worship and live in spirit and in truth. When people see me, I'd like them to know that I've been with Jesus.

Please hear this prayer as the expression of my heart. Father, separate me from the pretender who's deep down inside. Amen.

Be Consistent from the Inside Out

The good news is that God is vitally interested in answering your prayer. God knows what needs to happen next. Your job is to surrender. Not believe, not accept, not even commit, but surrender: "God, please possess me, inhabit me, do with me whatever you wish." If that is your prayer, God will carry you from there.

You can be free from needing to worry about what your boss, buddies, teacher, or friends think. Ultimately, I am going to stand before God, accountable to God for what I did with this incredible gift of life. The question you and I need to be asking as we go through this life is this: "Am I pleasing God? Is God pleased?"

Some people find great help from an accountability to Christian community. In the book of Acts, we see that the believers hung out together, day by day. They partied together. They took meals together in their houses. If I'm on the road where I might be tempted, I'd better be with a brother in Christ, each reminding the other of who owns and possesses us.

In the sidebar you'll see a living example of the value of accountability. As you read it, ask yourself who is in your group. You're not going to make it without peer support

Keelan Downtown: A Real Follower Who Asks Others to Keep Him Honest

I grew up just outside New York City and am a student at Messiah College, Grantham, Pennsylvania. I was an intern at Ginghamsburg.

At school, I meet once a week with three guys for discipleship. We get together and talk about what's going on in our lives and what God is doing. They know me and they know what's inside me. They know the depths of what's happening in my life. That's how they hold me accountable.

Because of the spiritual intimacy and trust we've built, we're able to challenge each other. In one sense, we get together and talk about our lives, but in another sense it's really "iron sharpening iron" (Prov. 27:17) as we grow in our faith together.

At times each of us thinks, *it would be so easy. . . .* Then we imagine trying to explain it to three friends willing to jump down your throat.

When I get together with these friends, I gain another perspective of who God is and what God's doing in my world. My point of view becomes more than a me-and-God thing. Instead, I see God's activity in community. I see it from the eyes of three other people, and I can get a much fuller perspective of the hand of God in my life.

like this. You will fall back into virtual religion without a group of encouragers to help you press forward.

Be Prepared That You Can't Outgive God

Trust, surrender, honesty, and truth may be hard "places" to hang out, but you'll find life here. You can be what God made you to be. You can quit worrying about what everyone thinks. You can be the real deal.

When God's Spirit touches your spirit, "He who supplies seed to the sower and bread for food will supply and multiply your seed for sowing and increase the harvest of your righteousness" (2 Cor. 9:10). God is unlimited. God has every resource of the universe at God's disposal. If God needs others, God can simply create them!

You and I will never regret the decision to become a real follower of Jesus.

The Holy Spirit releases all of the resources of God into a follower so we can release those same resources for God's purpose. God blesses you so you can be a stream through which blessings can flow to others—and no longer a dam that stops them from flowing.

All of those priceless resources are available to each of us if we are faithful to live out God's purpose. You and I will never regret the decision to become a real follower of Jesus.

Discussion Questions

1. What does "being a pretender on the inside" mean to you? Why did Mike Slaughter press so hard on this matter of "the pretender inside each of us"?

2. Has there been a time in your journey with God when being a real follower was clearly your first priority? If so, what were some of the good things God did through you?

3. Has God showed you an area of pretending that he wants to purify you from? How have you invited God to work in that area of your life?

> *4. If you're meeting in a group, ask how you can pray for one another. Pray together.*

Joining the Movement

 What could your entire church do to challenge and change the culture around you?

Example: Are you in a group, such as a home group, care circle, or small Sunday school class, where it would be appropriate for various members to tell their story? Few spiritual gatherings are more special than those where people tell their honest story of how God has set them free. Why not obtain the necessary permissions for the next four to six meetings to begin with various participants giving a short account of their journey as a Jesus follower? If possible, set the stage by going first! Maybe practice telling your life story in front of a close friend before saying it to the group.

Example: How could even more lives be touched through the lives God has already transformed in your congregation? If your church has a cassette ministry, why not make a special collection of life-transforming stories? Many churches find such tapes to be their most popular and widely distributed. If your church has a video ministry, why not capture someone's story on tape, edit it, and ask your pastor if it would be appropriate to use as part of a Sunday celebration or outreach event?

Afterword

Our job is to create a community of revolutionary people who see and understand themselves as servants of God. We connect people to their highest calling and gift.

Programs do not change people. The Jesus revolution will be demonstrated through a new community. God's plan has always been to work through a living group of people who demonstrate on earth what God has envisioned in heaven: reconciling people with God's revolutionary love, and with each other.

If you have never experienced a transforming personal relationship with God through Jesus Christ, why not ask God to bring you to a faith community of friends who can help you make the next step? Then go for it! *Get Real!*

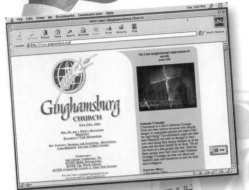

COME AND EXPERIENCE

Difference-Making
Seminars and
Workshops

Michael Slaughter,
Lead Pastor

Ginghamsburg